SCENES FROM

HITLER'S
"1000-YEAR REICH"

SCENES FROM

HITLER'S
"1000-YEAR REICH"

Twelve Years of Nazi Terror
and the Aftermath

KERRY WEINBERG, PH.D.

 Prometheus Books

59 John Glenn Drive
Amherst, New York 14228-2197

Published 2003 by Prometheus Books

Inquiries should be addressed to
Prometheus Books
59 John Glenn Drive
Amherst, New York 14228–2197
VOICE: 716–691–0133, ext. 207
FAX: 716–564–2711
WWW.PROMETHEUSBOOKS.COM

07 06 05 04 03   5 4 3 2 1

Library of Congress Cataloging-in-Publication Data

Weinberg, Kerry.
    Scenes from Hitler's "1000-year Reich" : twelve years of Nazi terror and the aftermath / Kerry Weinberg.
        p. cm.
    Includes bibliographical references and index.
    ISBN 1–59102–045–X
    1. Weinberg, Kerry. 2. Holocaust survivors—Germany—Biography. 3. Jews—Germany—Trier—Biography. 4. National soicialism— Psychological aspects. 5. Hitler, Adolf, 1889–1945. I. Title: Scenes from Hitler's "Thousand-year Reich". II. Title.

DS135.G5W42 2003
940.53'18'092—dc21
[B]   2002037131

Printed in Canada on acid-free paper

To the memory
of my mother
and
to all the genius, creativity,
and nobility of mind annihilated
by Hitler's henchmen

There are stars whose radiance is visible on earth though they have long been extinct. There are people whose brilliance continues to light the world though they are no longer among the living. These lights are particularly bright when the night is dark. They light the way to humanity.

—Hannah Senesh

CONTENTS

List of Illustrations   11

Introduction   13

1. Before Hitler   19

2. A Jewish Girl in an Aryan School   25

3. The *Kristallnacht* and After—
   Düsseldorf Epilogue   39

4. In Vichy France   61

5. Nazi Germany from an Aryan Perspective—
   Himmler's "Eugenic" Baby Factories   65

6. Life at Auschwitz   79

CONTENTS

7. The Loot   85

8. Survivors of the Inferno Tell Their Stories   89

9. After the Liberation   105

10. Between Palestine and Israel   113

11. Six National Anthems!   121

12. Visiting Jewish Memorials in "New" Europe   135

13. Interlude in Las Palmas   143

14. Afterword   151

Notes   157

Frequently Used Abbreviations and Foreign Words   163

Works Cited   165

Index of Names   167

LIST OF ILLUSTRATIONS

1. My parents after their wedding, June 1913

2. My parents about 1933

3. My father as soldier, WWI

4. My National Political Training class at the Aryan High School, January 1934

5. One of my classes in Tel Aviv

6. My sister, five months pregnant, and her husband, Henri, after their wedding, Vichy France

7. My sister, the perfect "Aryan" image

8. My sister and her husband, 1945, Vichy France

9. One of Himmler's dedicated officers
   lines up Polish civilians

10. A civilian round-up from the Lodz ghetto,
    to be transported or killed

11. Early Nazism in practice

12. Mussolini visiting Hitler—their budding friendship

13. Midnight rally glorifying military might

14. Hitler touring Paris—his sole visit to the
    French capital

INTRODUCTION

Who was the originator of the Holocaust who intoxicated the two nations of Greater Germany? In World War II, when living above ground became unsafe, the dictator, from the safety of his bunker, initiated the murder of countless more millions. No one knows exactly the staggering number of millions of lives worldwide that he caused to be lost.

According to the record, he had sprung from an incestuous marriage. His mother, Klara Pölzl, worked as a maid in her relative's house from age sixteen on. In his biography of Hitler, Ian Kershaw states that Alois Hiedler or Hüttler, who later changed his name to Hitler, twenty-three years her senior, was her second cousin. Judging by the family tree, it is more likely that he was her uncle, and she was known to have usually called him "Uncle."[1] She was pregnant with Alois's fourth child when they overcame an Austrian law against incestuous marriages and got married in 1885.

Adolf was born in 1889, one of six children. He and his youngest sister were the only ones who survived early childhood. Adolf apparently had an unhappy childhood, being frequently severely beaten by his violent, often drunken father, who resented the boy's unwillingness to settle down to any serious work, insisting that he wanted to become a great artist, without, however, exhibiting any talent.[2] "In den Krankheiten der Kinder offenbaren sich die Lastern der Eltern," we read in *Mein Kampf*[3] ("The children's diseases reveal their parents' vices"), although this is mentioned in a different context, not related to his own childhood.

Growing up, Hitler was trying frantically to find a scapegoat for the ills around him; he began blaming everything on the Jews, who seemed different from other residents: capitalism and Marxism, the Social-Democratic Party, prostitution and syphilis, economical downturns, poverty and war, and "degenerative" modern art were all their fault, he claimed.[4] Later, he wrote, "If the Jews did not exist, we would have to invent them."

In contrast to Hitler's dysfunctional background, both my parents originated from stable, conservative, reputable families. "Most mistakes are made in a hurry," was the motto of many well-established German-Jewish families, such as my parents and grandparents. After Hitler's take-over, the fatal mistake was to continue as usual and wait.

The Jews who still lived in Germany, Austria, and many other European countries in late 1941 knew that there was no longer an escape; they also knew that deportation meant inhuman suffering and death. In the invaded countries, most were taken by surprise and rounded up for deportation or immediate massacre. In Germany and Austria they were officially informed beforehand of their "resettlement" date.

My parents and most of my relatives would never have committed suicide because it is strictly against the Jewish religion. There were relatively few individuals, and probably one group in Belgium, who did not show up at the railroad station on the scheduled evening. With the exception of Rabbi Leo Baeck, who refused to leave his congregation in Berlin and was deported with his remaining flock, most rabbis and their families had left and found refuge in other countries or on distant continents. The vacancy was usually filled by one person who assumed the leadership of the dwindled Jewish community. One wonders why the leaders did not choose to guide the unfortunate remnant of their congregation to follow the example of Massadah,* knowing that they would be exposed to unspeakable torture and murder.

The genocide of the many millions of Jews was well prepared and organized with the help of large industries producing poisons of mass destruction. Methodical organizing has always been known to be an indigenous German characteristic. That mastery was used in the diabolical, systematic extermination process against the Jews. Auschwitz alone, without even counting hundreds of other death camps and massacre sites, has been called "the world's greatest battlefield . . . considering the number of those who died there."[5]

However, the enormity of the crime went far beyond

---

*In 73 C.E. the Jews, trapped by the Romans under Gessius Florus in their mountain fortress Massadah, rather than suffer torture, murder, and shame, committed mass suicide.

physical extinction. It involved the wealth of productivity in all cultural areas which was snuffed out, and which was not permitted to unfold in the more than one million children who perished—talents in science, the humanities, engineering, inventions, art, and the like.

Even those who were saved through emigration could not always develop and live up to their potential due to unforeseen circumstances, hardships, inadequate preparation, lack of adaptability, and absence of support from their families, which had been torn apart.

Thus the workings of creative minds in intellectual fields, to which the Jews have been contributing throughout recorded history, and particularly since their emancipation, were lost to the world in Hitler's genocide.

Like myself, there are many people the world over, not only surviving family members of the countless millions of victims, who hoped that humankind had learned a lesson form the Holocaust, and that the knowledge of that horror would prevent future dehumanized actions. That hope has been shattered.

A new specter is haunting the Western world. Megalomaniacs are threatening civilized nations and even their own people. While all this is being debated, there seems to be one constant: the unabated hatred of the Jews and the anti-Israel sentiment. This attitude is also spread among the allegedly enlightened Western nations.

While living in a rather peaceful environment as a child, I learned that when anything went wrong on this globe, like the plague in former centuries, economic downturns, war or famine, blame it on the Jews! During the pre-Hitler years, I read about monstrous anti-Jewish actions and pogroms, which made me turn to Zionism as the ideal solution against anti-Semitism. However, after the turbulent Middle East events of recent years, even some staunch Zionists are desperate when Palestinian fanatics, whose culture is steeped in blood, mutilate their own neighbors who object to having their children trained as "martyrs," blowing themselves to bits as suicide bombers.

In the present Armageddon, the war of civilization against terrorism, oppression, superstition, prejudice, and retrogression, perhaps good will prevail over evil, as history has proven from time to time. But in the meantime, nobody can predict the shattering cost of human lives and suffering.

ONE

BEFORE HITLER

After World War I, under the Versailles Treaty, the left Rhineland was under French occupation until 1930. In that year, the residents were to vote whether to become part of the French mainland or to be reintegrated in Germany and dispose of the French occupying forces, while maintaining that part of the country as a demilitarized zone.

In the 1920s official announcements were made in both languages. From early childhood on, the melodious sounds of the French language were particularly attractive to me and literally music to my ears, and they remained so throughout my life. One of my first childhood memories involved the soldiers of the Foreign Legion in their colorful outfits galloping wildly through the streets of my native city of Trier. Sometimes catching sight of them through the window fascinated my older sister and me; but women and children, for reasons which we understood many years later, avoided venturing out into the streets after dark and walked brisquely going about their business during the daytime.

Jews were totally emancipated and integrated and considered themselves as patriotic German citizens of Jewish faith, distinguished only in their religion from Protestants and Catholics, the latter being the vast majority in our city and the surrounding rural areas. Jews were generally known to be law-abiding, reliable, hard-working citizens, charitable and of high moral standards. They were welcomed to settle down in any neighborhood. When my sister and I were approaching our midteens and our family moved to a larger, more comfortable apartment, all the neighbors were very friendly. My Orthodox parents adhered openly and without restraint to our Jewish rituals. Our Sabbath and holiday songs, which we children sang with gusto, were heard all over our non-Jewish neighborhood and sometimes admired, judging by occasional complimentary remarks. My parents were greeted and treated with respect in the house and outside and felt completely safe. Noticing the mezuzoth on our doorposts, carrying the Sukkoth (Harvest Festival) paraphernalia, the *lulov* and *etrog*, to the synagogue, disposing of our sins symbolically in the Mosel River before the High Holidays never created a problem. Such rituals were viewed with mild interest, just as we noticed, but did not pay much attention to, the different customs of other religious affiliates.

Not all members of our congregation were as strictly observant as our family; but we went about our various religious rituals unostentatiously, for example, no sports or work on Saturdays and holidays, no bicycle rides or tramways, no touching of heat and electricity, no writing, and so on. Until Hitler's takeover, we had a live-in maid from a Mosel village, who was trained to tend to the utilities and other chores.

Thus living as an Orthodox Jewish family and proud Germans looking back at several generations of statehood did not present any problem, nor did it require any cover-up in our Westernized border city, where we shared much of the lifestyle and daily concerns about basic questions with others. Our religious preoccupation was centered in the synagogue, as theirs was in their churches. While my parents socialized only with Jewish friends, they frequently chatted with other neighbors. My father's business customers, mostly from the countryside, were almost all non-Jews. If anyone purchased his textiles or bedding on the installment plan and was severely delinquent in his payment by contract, the law took its course, my father being represented by a team of (incidentally Jewish) lawyers, or representing his own case.

At school I loved everything. The only classes that were separate were those in religious instruction. Ours were administered by our rabbi—Hungarian-born, aloof, unhappily estranged from his congregation and without much rapport with us students—and consisted of silent or out loud reading from a history book. In addition, we had more lively classes, officially unconnected with our school, taught by the cantor on rituals and Hebrew terminology. Priests and ministers taught the students of other affiliations.

The only anti-Semitic remark that I remember from my early childhood was an ugly slogan printed on a large poster during an election period, when a Jewish party leader ran for office.

A major disaster occurred in our family, the causes and drastic consequences of which I understood only many years later when I was older. In the skyrocketing inflation that followed World War I in the 1920s, many German people suffered grave financial losses. My father, who had accumulated great wealth as a young man and provided handsome dowries to his three younger sisters so that they were all well married, added my mother's substantial dowry to his own assets when he himself tied the knot. The foolish ancient custom, which had forced the famous George Sand after leaving her husband to walk pennilessly into the world with her small child, still persisted at the time of my parents' marriage: the dowry was handed over in cash to the bridegroom. Despite repeated pleadings by my grandfather, descended from many wealthy, astute business generations, my obstinate father continued to invest unwisely in uninsured banks. Warning telegrams came too late: He lost every penny of the family fortune, one of the largest in our city. Of course, he could never again show his face to my grandfather after that.

In our childhood, my sister and I usually spent our summer vacation with our maternal grandparents in Alsfeld, a town in Hessen with many quaint medieval buildings and a large Jewish community, half of whose members were related one way or another. Many ran a thriving business, one relative was a physician, another a museum curator. My grandparents owned a large house with a huge fruit and vegetable garden and other properties, and lots of noisy ducks with their offspring in the courtyard. My grandparents were very close to their non-Jewish tenants and neighbors, who obviously valued their friendship and advice. There were always other young relatives visiting, usually students much older than we, and there was often something exciting going on, so different from our city life. Each visitor had an interesting family history. We roamed around freely in the garden, admired the ducks, and were always kept busy.

My mother's younger sister, Aunt Ida, got married several years after the war, and her husband opened a wine and liquor distillery in the basement, which we were sometimes allowed to watch from a safe distance. The following year, there was a lively little baby boy, Manfred, another fascination.

Only rarely, years before the advent of Hitler, did we overhear a subdued conversation among the adult relatives about an anti-Semitic remark or incident, unlike anything that we could remember from our border city; we soon forgot about it.

We learned that both my mother and my aunt, two years apart, around ages eighteen and twenty, had been sent for one year to a distinguished Jewish *Pensionat*, a sort of boarding school for refined young women, where they were trained in all the accoutrements necessary for their future station as perfect Jewish married ladies and hostesses. They learned gourmet cooking, baking, table manners, embroidery, literature, and dancing, and visited operas and theaters. No doubt it was an enjoyable time for all participants. The syllabus apparently did not include decision making, nutritional values, or watching the health and well-being of those under their care. Of course, there was no TV, no radio, no Dr. Laura at that time that the young women, once married, could fall back on. Later on, my mother would often sing operatic libretti to us children when we were waiting on Sabbath evening for my father to return from the service. The theaters and oper(ett)as instilled Bovarisme-like dreams in her for many years to come, as I understood in my adult life.

There were also two uncles, brothers younger than my mother and aunt, with whom those of us who survived the Nazi regime kept in touch whenever possible after we were scattered all over the world.

TWO

A JEWISH GIRL IN AN ARYAN SCHOOL

S aturday, April 1, 1933, in Trier, a city of 100,000, very near the West German borders of Luxemburg and France. Though it was my birthday, I expected nothing noteworthy to happen—school as usual, six days a week, except Sundays. The difference from the weekdays was that, growing up in an Orthodox home, my elder sister and I walked the long way to and from school instead of using the trolley car through the inner city or, in dry weather, riding our bikes along the parks; and, of course, we did not write on the Sabbath.

My sister, promptly after her high-school graduation, which coincided with Hitler's takeover of the government, had already left for her carefully prepared enrollment at Strasbourg University. One of her last classroom experiences

A portion of this text appeared as a series in *Martyrorn and Resistance* (New York: International Society for Yad Vashem, 1997) September/October pp. 5, 15 and November/December pp. 6, 13. Also given as a lecture at the Rockland Center for Holocaust Studies, May 1997. It is used with the publisher's permission.

25

was her new biology teacher making her stand on a desk to demonstrate her typically Aryan features and coloring![1] On that Saturday I walked home alone through the familiar narrow one-way streets of the business section, bordered by mostly Jewish-owned shops and department stores. The usually crowded, very lively area had turned into a ghost city: All the stores were closed, the streets deserted. The entrances were guarded by uniformed storm troopers, and huge posters displaying predatorial caricatures of Jews and slogans from *Der Stürmer*, the Nazi newspaper, covered the walls and windows everywhere. While my Catholic classmates, with whom I had been very chummy until recently, had probably been prepared for that boycott and hate demonstration in their new organization, the BDM, *Bund Deutscher Mädchen* (League of German Girls)—the counterpart of the Hitler Youth for boys—I, the only Jewish girl in my class and one of two in our girls' school, was completely shocked. Was that how anyone could conceive of me, the popular student in our high school?

Up to then, success had engendered success; I loved all my idealistic teachers, to whom I felt closer than to my parents, who provided my religious background and rituals; I had been playacting in mostly French roles, loved math, languages, music, painting, writing poetry. My classmates had been in and out of our home and I in theirs. I had felt as patriotic as any of them, as no doubt did my parents— my father, a slender, blond, blue-eyed,[2] sports-loving business man, a World War I veteran, and my mother, from a large, well-known, very religious land-owning family. Our teachers had always instilled the philosophy in us that any potential and talent had to be utilized for the benefit of the country as much as for oneself. That day, my world collapsed. Life, which had always been so rich, full of promise and challenges, ceased to make sense.

I came home, dazed. The atmosphere was gloomy. My parents had, of course, witnessed the horrible displays on their way home from the synagogue. Now, as later, they hoped to avert the doom through prayer. In accordance with a new law, our live-in Aryan maid of many years had been dismissed. That lonely weekend, my sister gone and none of my friends showing up, I had plenty of time to ponder what the ambience in class would be like and to wonder why none of my friends had warned me of the planned demonstration.

The day before, my parents had received a letter from Ipswich, England, containing an urgent invitation to have me finish my schooling, followed by later university attendance, in the home of Johnny's parents. Johnny was a divinity student, with a minor in drama and acting, who had been the last one of several English students hosted by us for the summer months. Contrary to my ease at foreign languages, my sister—less proficient—had left it to me to escort and direct him and to attend his performances.

Perhaps my parents never answered that letter, being preoccupied with *kashruth*, dietary laws, convinced that the situation would "blow over." My father's business still continued at that time. Besides, many Jews who still had their livelihood felt they were at a safe distance from the ugly rumors occasionally heard about events in the inland area and Berlin, in contrast to our border city, until recently under French occupation according to the Versailles Treaty.

The only ones who put their homes on the market in

1933 were two households, both old Zionists, who had immediately been deprived of their licenses as a physician and a dentist, respectively, and early received their immigration permits to Palestine. Their leaving ended our musical trio. The physician's son later made his career as a violinist in the Israeli Philharmonic Orchestra. I played the piano, having already given a concert of a Hayden sonata and a Handel fugue at age thirteen, which earned me some flattering newspaper reviews. And the third in our group was a brilliant teenage cellist. My hopes to make either the piano or mathematics my career were shattered by emigration.

To my surprise and relief, everyone that Monday was casual, friendly, and seemingly unembarrassed; no one mentioned the outrageous boycott. Only one girl, who had sometimes seemed a bit jealous of me, praised the "new spirit" enthusiastically during the following weeks and gloated over my restraint and my absence from extracurricular activities. In after-school hours, I noticed the abrupt withdrawal of all my Aryan friends.

Outwardly, the demanding schedule in school, where I was also enrolled in the optional Latin, Spanish, and Greek philosophy, continued with unabated respect and friendliness to me by my teachers and most classmates. I was tactfully exempt from raising my right arm for the "Heil Hitler" salute at the beginning of each lesson and from joining in the Horst-Wessel Song, which replaced the former national anthem. The only one who stared at me disapprovingly at first was the young math teacher, who, against his well-known convictions, joined in paying tribute to the dictator. In the school chorus, where I was the heart of the alto section with my well-developed vocal chords, I remained silent at Nazi songs which, for instance, replaced *"Deutschland über alles von der Etsch bis an den Belt . . ."* by "Today Germany, Tomorrow the World!"[3]

In January of 1934, the students of our three parallel classes were ordered "without exception" to undergo "national-political training" in the icy Eifel Mountains for two weeks. About seventy of us were assigned bunk beds in the dorms of a youth hostel, all being under the supervision of our nature-loving biology teacher. The schedule was rough, following the motto "Strength through Adversity, Wisdom through Suffering": a wake-up call before sunrise, then half an hour's aerobics in an unheated gym, followed by a basic breakfast consisting of peasant ryebread and a brew of postum "coffee" with milk in a now-heated room, then a two-hour hike on the snow- and ice-covered mountain. Returning to the hostel from the military-style march, there was a lengthy session in "Racial Theory and Anthropology," which indoctrinated students about the superiority of the master race and the inferiority and subhuman characteristics of Jews, gypsies, colored people, and Slavs. Along with Gerda, another Jewish girl, I was excluded from these classes. (Years later, I learned that Gerda died mysteriously shortly after her emigration to North Africa.)

Everyone was now ravenously hungry and looking forward to the highlight of the day, the early afternoon dinner. By special permission, my mother sent me packages containing kosher sausage and canned peas or the like every few days. Hitler's gang would have been outraged to witness the delight with which my former friends vied to sit next to me and relish a sample of my kosher snacks. If anyone had informed the authorities of their love of Jewish food, they would no doubt have been punished. Surprisingly, no one got sick during that strenuous sojourn, including my frail self, whereas at home I often suffered from colds during the winter.

After one week, our guide approached me before my free period during her Racial Anthropology session and asked me to compose a poem and set it to music, to greet a head administrator, who was visiting with his entourage that afternoon. She apparently knew that I had written poetry on various occasions. So I composed a seven-line poem to the tune of the English national anthem. After her class, she looked it over and approved. No typewriter or piano being available in that primitive setup, she asked me to select a dozen girls from our school chorus to make copies and learn to sing it.

That afternoon, Professor Kohn, a charming Catholic priest with a mysterious Jewish name, arrived, escorted by half a dozen other administrators. My song addressing the distinguished head started with the word "Führer." Unlike my schoolmates, I was not aware as yet that Hitler was routinely referred to and addressed as "Führer." To my unspeakable embarrassment, all right arms shot up at that word! They were lowered again when everybody realized that this eulogistic address was directed at Dr. Kohn.

The short revival of close friendship with my Aryan classmates ended in the aftermath of this wintry mountain interlude. School continued more or less as usual, with songs constantly focused on war, conquests, the flag, bravery, the ultimate glory of sacrificing one's life for the Führer and the fatherland. The refrain of one popular song was, "Volk, ans Gewehr!"* My social orientation had to be concentrated now on Jewish circles. I became interested in Zionism and was soon active in a leadership role to assist youngsters to secure training positions (*hachsharah*) preparing them for immigration to rural Palestine kibbutzim. I placed one of them, from my uncle's orphanage, for an apprenticeship with a local Jewish carpenter, and I was able to have the boy established with my own family and some others for his Sabbath and holiday meals. (He lost his life at age twenty-eight in Nahariah, fighting in the 1948 Israeli War of Independence.) I was fortunate in saving several lives by my endeavors, as I was told many years later when meeting some of my protégés again.

Previous spare-time activities, like theater and opera subscriptions, which my sister and I had enjoyed since our preteens; skating and canoeing with non-Jewish company; occasional visits to fascinating trials at the law-courts on school-free days, often interrupted by a judge objecting to children in the audience; my father taking us on early Sunday morning mountain hikes—all this ceased abruptly, after huge signs sprang up everywhere, "Jews Undesirable," "No Admittance to Jews," and the like. Instead, after practically all the other Jewish teenagers had left the area, there was the Jewish Youth Organization, whose members were much older than I.

My teachers continued in their loyalty to me up to my graduation with math as my special elective, and perhaps some of them even jeopardized their position by their fairness to me. A few decades later, during a visit in Trier, I learned that our high-school faculty had written a letter to my parents about their successful attempts to gain my

---

*"Nation, up to arms!"

admission for studies at Cologne University. My parents never informed me of that letter.

The beginning of the end came in 1935, when a rapid succession of new nationwide laws against Jews, and any Aryans associated with them in any way, brought a brutal wake-up call to those Jews who had lived in the false hope that in our distant border area of devoted Catholic inhabitants the situation would be different from the disturbing events in the interior cities and the eastern part of Germany, and that life would continue to be tolerable for Jews. German Jews were deprived of their citizenship rights and no longer had recourse to the law. They could no longer own real estate nor, in most cities, any business. Firms with Jewish owners were gradually closed down. In rare cases, when there was an opportunity, a Jewish owner found an Aryan partner and continued to conduct transactions under that partner's name for some time. Overnight, every Jew became a statistic. Even my father must have understood that there was no longer any life for Jews in Germany.

Rumors spread about increasing abuse of Jews, especially in the capital. I overheard a whispered conversation in which a neighboring widow confided in my mother, complaining bitterly that her brilliant daughter, a recent university graduate, could not get a job, having refused to join the party. Stealing and violence were now not only legal but praised as heroic and patriotic. Outspoken religious leaders, like a certain priest from our city, were branded as treasonous "panic-mongers" who spread "horror stories." Their parishioners soon learned that their pastors had disappeared in concentration camps. Some frightened churchgoers whispered a new prayer in the Trier vernacular: "Lieber Gott, mach' mich stumm,/ Dass ich nicht nach Dachau kumm!" ("Dear God, make me dumb,/ So I won't be sent to Dachau!")

This is how the dictator and his cohorts won over even the staunchest critics and dissidents: The difference between being a party member or not meant either social acceptance, success, promotion, and feathering one's nest with the stolen Jewish properties and positions; or starving, being a social outcast, and incarceration. One of those who early reaped the benefits of the New Order was a former classmate of mine, who dropped out of school and became a seamstress to help feed her many younger siblings, her father being unemployed. Now she walked tall and proud, her father having been reinstated in a job and her siblings being subsidized in food, clothing, and health care from the third child down, according to a new law, as soon as her father joined the party union, the NSDAP.

Shortly after the proclamation of the new laws, my father was waylaid and beaten up by a customer who owed him substantial amounts of money for merchandise being paid by installments. Soon after this assault, my father suffered an acute glaucoma attack, which required surgery.

In the capital and other cities, the works of all Jewish authors past and present, and those of some modern non-Jews, were burned in huge bonfires as "Degenerative Art." Surprisingly, one very popular German song, "Die Lorelei," based on the text of the nineteenth-century Jewish poet Heinrich Heine, continued to reverberate throughout the country and to appear in student textbooks. It was overlooked by Hitler and his henchmen; knowledge of the humanities by representatives of the Third Reich was considered worthless and usually less than basic.

Meanwhile, the parades of stomping storm troopers increased, as did the speeches and posters of the grotesque-looking fascist trio—the undersized, ugly Propaganda Minister Goebbels, the overweight Field Marshal Goering (with his insatiable appetite for stolen Jewish and foreign antique treasures), and the dictator himself, always screaming inflammatory threats and promises in his heavy Austrian accent.

I later understood why my parents had been repeatedly called and urged by our school administration, while the National-Socialist Party had been gathering momentum, to have me skip some classes in order to graduate earlier. My ultraconservative father, who had always been very partial to my elder sister, stubbornly refused, to avoid humiliation to her, an average student; and my all-too-passive mother left important decisions to him. In an Orthodox family like ours, the second child was supposed to be a boy, and my father did not hide resenting a second daughter. Having had no guidance counselors like modern American schools nor all the modern media, youngsters then were not as critical as today's youth. One cannot choose one's parents nor expect all of them to be worldly wise, intelligent, and sophisticated. One might expect, however, that they bestow an equal share of care, fairness, planning, and assets on their children. Unfortunately, my parents paid the price for their unequal treatment of their children, as did I, like the victims of the medieval custom of primogeniture in certain aristocratic circles, where all the interest and assets were focused on the eldest son.

Meanwhile, having graduated from high school with *summa cum laude*—the only one of three classes, despite

Hitler—I soon became involved with an intelligent bon-vivant, twelve years my senior, being flattered that he singled me out with his attentions, as were my parents. However, it would apparently not have been a marriage made in Heaven, for after a while I fell out of love.

Jews being barred from all public entertainment and cultural events, the newly established *Jüdische Kulturbund* (Jewish Culture Council) offered older folks an occasional concert or play to look forward to and prevented their total isolation and intellectual deterioration. It also provided a very modest income, albeit short-lived, to the ousted Jewish actors and musicians. On the other hand, it may have lulled to sleep some people's sense of the ever-tightening noose and the impending disaster.

In late 1936 I enrolled at the Würzburg Jewish Teachers College, which was focused on rabbinical studies, and cantoral training for boys, and offered little on teacher preparation and classroom management. While the demanding ultra-Orthodox atmosphere was a spiritual bastion isolating students and faculty against the increasingly brutal outside reality, this isolation by its very nature prevented its enrollees from planning ahead, thus causing several individuals who were left behind to be trapped in the ultimate catastrophe.

An advantage of my enrollment was that I was able, with official permission, to free some of my sister's sizable blocked bank account for my monthly expenses at the teachers college. In the process, I saved certain amounts regularly for my parents. My hope that my sister could and would file an application for my parents' temporary admission to France proved too optimistic. Knowing that my father would do nothing to transfer funds out of the country (except the legal way for my sister's living expenses, still possible at that time), I took this necessary evil upon myself. Although it was very dangerous, especially on the left Rhineland, I took the risk and secured some money for them via a source near the Dutch border that I had discovered. I also set about finding and purchasing quality furniture for my sister's lift to be sent to France, where she had become engaged recently. The furniture had to be "used," according to a German law, and I had it soiled a bit to make it look old!

During a short recess in 1937, I and another girl made reservations at Jewish tourist houses and kosher restaurants, which were advertised in a Jewish newspaper, and set out on a bicycle tour to the Black Forest and along the Rhine River. All along the way we were faced with swastikas and huge signs, "Juden Unerwünscht!" and "Juden Ist der Eintritt Verboten!" ("Jews Undesirable!" and "Entry Forbidden to Jews!") Once, at night on a lonely road, we arrived at a Jewish tourist home where we had made a reservation. We found it closed, deserted. We were afraid and very hungry. But remembering the Nuremberg Statutes of September 1935, which deprived Jews of all legal rights, we did not dare to approach a private house. We were glad to make it back to the safety of our temporarily sheltered life on the college campus.

After attending college for a year and a half, I graduated, and until the *Kristallnacht* pogrom I taught for a few months in Düsseldorf, hoping to obtain my student certificate for Palestine soon, which was long overdue.

Many decades later I was asked by friends in Australia

during their election campaign about my opinion as to whether overtly anti-Semitic legislation would ever be possible in their country or in the United States. My answer was that I trust our Constitution and their laws would preclude such a danger. Some of my fellow executives of the B'nai B'rith Lodge wondered, if an anti-Semitic candidate were ever elected president of the United States, would the American Jews consider running away at once to start a new life in an unknown part of the world, or would we wait and see, as many Jews did in Germany?

THREE

THE KRISTALLNACHT AND AFTER

Düsseldorf Epilogue

I had my first teaching position at the Private Jewish School in the elegant city of Düsseldorf on the Rhine, where I was in charge of general subjects, the girls' gym, and adult evening classes in English and French. I had rented a furnished apartment, overlooking a park, on the third floor of a mansion owned by a judge's widow. She was a superb pianist, a very large lady, who occupied that huge building with her tiny, fragile housekeeper, equally erudite and refined. Their contrasting sizes made them a strange-looking pair. Along with half a dozen other patrons, I took my meals at a private kosher luncheonette run by a formerly Polish couple, now termed "without nationality," whose cooking, so different from our Western cuisine at home, I enjoyed. This enterprise offered them a modest income after their business, like that of most other Jewish owners, had been closed by the

---

Part of this chapter was published in *Jewish Frontier* (May/June 1987): 18–20. It is used with the publisher's permission.

Nazis. The other guests confided in me that they planned to cross the border into Holland soon and urged me to join them.

On November 9, 1938, I was the only one at the luncheonette. All the others had "left," I was told. I was waiting, with some apprehension, to hear from a friend in Berlin. Because of his Polish parentage and his status "without nationality," he could not find a job despite his good qualifications; his excellent operatic tenor voice made him earn some money by freelancing as a cantor. When I mentioned the matter to the friendly couple at the luncheonette, they sighed and turned away. A few days later I learned about the fate of thousands of Jewish immigrants from Eastern Europe who had sought refuge in Germany many years ago. They had been rounded up, packed onto cattle trains, and unloaded in the snowcovered forests of Zbondgin, a no-man's-land between Germany and Poland, to starve and freeze to death.

Around 3:00 A.M. of November 10, I was awakened by my landlady. Screams and a lot of commotion could be heard from the next building. My landlady told me that, in retaliation for an assassination attempt on the German ambassador in Paris, a former Düsseldorf resident, by Herschel Grünspan (his bullet killed a secretary), the Nazis were arresting Jews, demolishing Jewish homes and places of business, and burning synagogues. Later we learned that the young refugee had heard about the deportation of his parents into the icy border woods; and we saw the newspaper headlines ascribing the brutalities against the Jews to the *Volkswut* throughout Germany, the "spontaneous outburst of the public fury" (organized by Hitler and his henchmen). The screams from the next building grew louder, shots rang, then a woman's voice, "My God, he is dead!" The three of us tiptoed downstairs into the dark kitchen where we sat listening, waiting for the SS to smash the front door. At dawn, the fragile housekeeper made some coffee.

In the first dim November daylight, I looked out the window. The park seemed deserted. Putting on a hat and sunglasses to hide my not-so-Aryan-looking brown eyes and hair, I ventured out into the street and walked to the school. I found the place screened off by SS. A huge crowd was watching the fire rise from a large wing of the synagogue. No familiar face was in sight.

Wearily I headed back to my lodgings, thinking about my parents, my grandmother, and other relatives and friends, all scattered over different cities and towns; they all had staunchly believed that twentieth-century Germany could not for long deny basic rights to law-abiding Jewish citizens, many of whom had suffered injury and loss while fighting for their fatherland in World War I. Where were they to go now that one country after another had shut its gates to refugees from Nazi oppression?

A new horror scene awaited me as I approached the park. An enormous, noisy crowd had gathered outside my landlady's mansion. The SS were lifting the home's heavy furniture, piece after piece, over the wrought-iron balcony fence into the street. The crowd cheered with delight as the feet of the grand piano were caught on the railing, from which the instrument dangled. Only a few of the onlookers were silent and seemed thoughtful. The house was teeming with SS. The two ladies were nowhere to be seen. Were they alive, I wondered; had they been dragged to concentration camps, too? The entrance was guarded by SS men. I found a phone booth and dialed the number of my uncle and aunt in Wuppertal several times, but in vain. My parents had no phone. I then remembered that there was a small branch of the U.S. Consulate in Cologne and caught a train to that destination.

I arrived in midafternoon, two hours before closing time. In the tiny waiting room, there was hardly space for another person to stand. Most of the people there were men, no doubt trying to avoid arrest or deportation by the Nazis, and perhaps—like me—seeking a waiting number for emigration to the United States. My father had a cousin in New York City who had visited us many times with her husband and my father's uncle; she had offered my sister and me an affidavit.

People talked freely to each other, all burdened with a common fear. After some time, an usher called up the "German nationals," and I was admitted to see the consular assistant just before closing. Identification and my fluent English cut the formalities short. Since I was expecting my student certificate to Palestine, I was mainly interested in securing a waiting number for my parents. I was told, however, that waiting numbers had to be picked up personally. I do not recall how I persuaded the man in charge to make an exception, but I did get a number for my parents, too. The consular official advised me that since the quota was heavily overbooked, emigration to America could take more than a year; I should therefore try to find transit elsewhere in the meantime.

Those left in the waiting room were ushered out. Many settled down on the stairs or in dark corners behind the stairways. I did not dare go to a hotel for the night. I knew only one private address in Cologne—that of the fiancé of my sister's girlfriend. To my unspeakable relief, he answered the phone; he gave me travel instructions and offered to have me spend the night in his parents' apartment. Once there, I had a meal—I had not eaten all day—and went to sleep. Exhausted and worried, I asked no questions when the young man and his brother told me to use their room, since they were sleeping elsewhere. Decades later, when I met him again in the United States, he told me that an officer of the brownshirts (the *Sturmabteilung*) who had known his family for twenty years, had warned him of the planned arrest of all Jewish men in the "spontaneous fury of the populace" and had insisted that he and his brother spend the next few nights under the beds in the officer's own apartment.

The next morning I reached my aunt, Mrs. Rothschild, in Wuppertal, by phone. She was alone, she said, and would I *please* come over. When I arrived, she recounted the previous forty-eight hours: "Uncle Max [my mother's brother] has the flu and a high fever. He has his English visa and his train ticket but is too sick to travel. Yesterday morning at dawn the doorbell rang, the SS were there to arrest him. He was in bed a few yards away, with the bedroom door ajar. I said, very upset, 'Oh my God, he left for England two days ago with his exit permit, passport, and visa, and I haven't heard from him. Please, please tell me if anything happened to him! Did he have an accident? Please, I want to know?' They apparently did not like my hysteria and left. We were sure they would come back. So I got Max dressed, and his Christian partner, in whose name the business has been run for some time, drove him to his bungalow in the forest to stay for a few days until he can travel and things calm down."

I was amazed at her presence of mind. She had always pampered herself, never done any work. The consensus among my relatives had been that my uncle had married a toy: "They divide their tasks—he earns the money and she spends it." Now her daring had saved his life.

Over the phone we sent cautious telegrams to my parents in Trier and to my sister in Strasbourg. We did not know if women had also been, or would be, shipped to concentration camps. For the night's lodgings we went to my aunt's seamstress. I still remember the very soft mattress in which we sank, and the warm featherbed. The next morning, at the Rothschilds' apartment, we received a cable from my parents over the phone, stating that they were "healthy." Any contact with my uncle was out of the question until he had crossed the border. Although my aunt was unwilling to let me go, I was anxious to see what had happened to my parents and to my classes in Düsseldorf. Before I left, my aunt gave me a magazine and advised me to hold it before my face, pretending to read, while I waited for the train; or else, I should hide in the ladies' room.

At the station, I had close to an hour's wait before the next train to Düsseldorf. Soon after I sat down in the waiting room, I noticed a young SS man staring at me and then striding toward me. My aunt's magazine did not deter him. He stopped right opposite me and kept on staring. I was sure my last hour had come. The SS, *Schutz-Staffel* or protective division for Hitler's cohorts, was known to spell death and destruction to non-Aryans and dissidents wherever they appeared. To my disbelief, the man said in a normal tone of voice, "Such eyes you have—I have never seen such eyes! You must leave Germany soon. We were actually ordered to round up all Jews, not only the men, and ship them to concentration camps or across the Eastern border. It was technically not possible. It will come. You must leave. I tell you what: If you can't get out soon, here is my card. Call me, and I'll help you across the border into Holland, I promise."

I nodded consent. I had the impression that he was sincere. Was it possible that the dreaded uniform harbored a human being, I wondered. Perhaps he once had Jewish friends or classmates, or a Jewish sweetheart. But another fear came over me now. I had read that if an Aryan was seen in the company of a Jew of the opposite sex, the Jew was automatically accused of seduction and quickly executed. The man gave me a last glance, clicked his heels, and walked away. I did take the card, which I left with my parents before departing for England a few months later. I can't believe it would have helped them, though; the SS man would never have risked himself for a middle-aged Jewish couple.

In Düsseldorf I first went to the principal's apartment, where I found his wife, a home-economics teacher at our school. It was still closed, she said. Her husband had been taken to a concentration camp, along with many other Jewish men, on the night of November 9. She had sent their young son away to friends, where she hoped he would be safe for the time being, until they were able to emigrate to America. She told me that the SS had gone to the hospital where the boys' gym teacher, Polish-born, had just undergone emergency surgery. They were searching the hospital to pack him on a cattle train the day after the operation and deport him to freeze to death. The doctor and nurses hid him in a lab closet and told the SS that he had been discharged. As soon as he could stand on his feet (I learned years later), he swam across the icy Saar River. In 1942 he was captured in France and scheduled for deportation from Gours Transit Camp, but he managed to escape and join the underground, where he met his future wife, with whom he has been living in New York since 1949.

Stopping at my landlady's, I found the house completely emptied of its contents. They had moved to the upper floor, my lodgings, using the twin bed and a cot which I had noticed in one of the closets, along with some blankets. Both the distinguished ladies seemed surprisingly stoical. Not a word of sorrow or complaint did they utter. I urged them to flee across the Dutch border and practice "the art of survival," to which I was determined to subscribe. They declined, saying they were too old, and if they were to die, so be it. Neither of them had any surviving family. I sensed that they had decided to end their own lives. Hindsight taught the wisdom of those who stayed behind and chose this way out.

I packed my belongings and left sadly. Feeling like an old, old woman after the events of the last few days, I caught a late afternoon train to Trier, my hometown. The peaceful Mosel was meandering unperturbed through the familiar picturesque valley. In the evening, I arrived and walked the eight or nine blocks to my parents' place. The streets looked as usual, with several uniformed men strutting about. No Jewish person was to be seen. I focused my thoughts on my parents, hoping against hope to find things unchanged.

I found my mother aged, helpless—she had obviously lost a lot of weight—contrasted with the calm and equanimity of my father. All the beautiful furniture in the dining room, living room, family room, and bedrooms had been hacked to pieces with axes and sledgehammers, including my beloved piano; the precious china sets, crystal, the delicate Meissen figurines had been smashed to smithereens, the liquor poured on the carpets and embroidered tablecloths, which had been swept out of the dressers, the sideboard, and the china closet. A major earthquake could not have caused more damage. The *"Kristallnacht,"* routinely translated as "The Night of Broken Glass," is a historical understatement, a misnomer for that nationwide pogrom, in which a thousand persons were killed and many tens of thousands shipped to concentration camps, synagogues and schools burned, homes ransacked, and cemeteries desecrated.

I was very attached to my mother, who had all the social graces and ease of communication, but had not been close to my taciturn, deeply religious father, whom I had never understood. In the midst of all the destruction, which both my parents had been forced to witness, uncertain whether and when the murder weapons would descend on themselves, he had maintained his composure.

There was no time for me to grieve. I had matured rapidly in those last few days. Briefly, I reported what had happened to me and our relatives in Wuppertal. My mother gained some strength from my presence, and both my parents took comfort from the official U.S. waiting numbers. I found myself faced with the task of parenting my parents.

We decided to have the Jewish carpenter repair whatever furniture could be salvaged. Although my father's textile business had previously been liquidated by the Gestapo, my parents were still able to live modestly on their savings.

There were no young Jewish people left in our city. Many years after my parents' death, I learned that they had intercepted the English Consulate's letter addressed to me containing my student visa for immigration to Palestine. I was perturbed realizing in retrospect that, even after the terrible pogrom of November 1938, they were reluctant to let me go, until the men of the dwindled congregation took my father to task for neglecting the future of his younger daughter.

The prospect of arriving pennilessly in a foreign country made refugees contrive all sorts of devices, such as hiding precious stones or gold pieces in coat buttons or in an imperceptibly marked armchair leg of a furniture lift, or even rolled in a clew of woolen knitting yarn. Some got away with it. Those who didn't were executed, which was the only mode of penalty imposed by the authorities of Nazi "justice," often after torture.

The morning after my return I made an appointment with the carpenter. His place was one of the few that had been spared. Perhaps the perpetrators of the "spontaneous Aryan fury" did not know that he was Jewish.

My next stop, upon my mother's instruction, was at Mrs. S.'s apartment to buy some coffee. She lived with her aged mother and eked out a scant living by running a home luncheonette of the kind I knew from Düsseldorf. Trier being close to the Luxembourg and French borders, her place was frequented by many who tried to flee Germany using forged papers. Her husband was in jail—no reason given. She told me that a few days earlier, at 2:00 A.M., the bell rang; outside stood the Gestapo chief, sleek, elegant, soft-spoken. He offered her the freedom of her husband in exchange for her spying on her patrons and turning in those who planned to cross the border with forged papers. There was nothing one could say to comfort the desperate lady. Years later I learned that her husband was reported to have hanged himself in prison, and she and her mother had perished in Auschwitz.

During the next few months, I took private lessons in conversational Hebrew. I had been told, "To prepare for a teaching career in America, learn Hebrew; for Palestine, English." Secretly at night I learned a practical trade from a neighboring lady hatter, a devout Catholic, secretly anti-Nazi like many Catholics. My Palestine student certificate did not appear. So when my uncle sent me an ad from London for a maid-and-governess job, I applied and was accepted. While waiting for the formalities to be completed, I pleaded with my sister—unfortunately, in vain—to apply for temporary admission of our parents to France on the basis of their U.S. waiting number.

Before leaving, I gave my parents some lessons in English, so they would have a foundation on which to continue on their own in the textbook I gave them—one lesson per week. My father seemed particularly perceptive and eager to study the language.

In May of 1939 I left for England. Like many other German and Austrian girls who sought refuge in English domestic positions, I knew little about housekeeping and less about cooking, but I learned on the job. Like France and some other European countries, England sometimes granted those with a U.S. waiting number a transit visa. Soon after my arrival in London, I obtained the necessary forms for my parents' admission to England, and I often sat till deep into the night, after an exhausting day of rigorous physical exertion, filling out the forms; but it was too late.

I listened fearfully to the BBC speeches of Oswald Mosley, the British National-Socialist propagandist, especially when, about one month after my arrival, he announced a parade through London's business center. On that day, the hardy Jewish young men of the metropolis were waiting for the marchers in a long receiving line, armed with kitchen and garden utensils. The parade was promptly nipped in the bud, and the demonstrators dispersed quickly.

Just before the outbreak of World War II, a cousin of mine from Alsfeld, a small town in Hessen, arrived in England with a children's transport. Having been exposed to frequent anti-Semitic remarks at school, his parents had sent him to the private Jewish school in Frankfurt. At age fifteen, he started an apprenticeship with a Jewish locksmith in a village near Giessen to learn a trade for emigration. On the morning of November 10, all the Jewish homes there having been destroyed at night, he phoned a Jewish family in his hometown, who told him he could *not* come home. With the money he had borrowed from the locksmith's family, he bought a ticket to reach a relative near the Dutch border, when he was suddenly beaten up and thrown to the ground, bleeding from a head wound. He was then put in a prison cell filled with men, all with badly swollen, bleeding, bruised faces, resulting from brutal beatings and pistol-whippings.

After a nightlong busride, they were given some water

and bread and arrived at the Buchenwald KZ, where they had to run the gauntlet between rows of SS, and then had to stand at attention all day, closely watched, beaten and mistreated if they relaxed their posture. Beards were torn out, eyeglasses smashed, and those who wore medals from World War I were particularly assaulted. Weakened diabetics, heart patients, and the like were beaten to the ground. There were no latrines yet. Whoever had to relieve himself had to do so anywhere and was beaten up. Machine guns were often heard. All heads were shaved. On one occasion, he recognized his father, and the two met. After two weeks, he being clearly the youngest in the camp, he heard his name called, and having contributed to the collection for the "Winter Aid" and lied about his headwound (saying he had clumsily hit himself), he was released. His father was freed two weeks later. One man, having lost one eye when beaten in the face, was never released and died at the camp, as we heard later. Before the inmates were freed, they were ordered never to say a word at home or abroad about their experiences at the camp, otherwise they would be back fast! His father, fighting for the fatherland in World War I, had been captured by the French and imprisoned in a prisoner of war (POW) camp until 1920. The atrocities to which father and son were exposed by the fatherland at Buchenwald, and the hair-raising butchery which they witnessed, made the harsh treatment by his French captors seem gentle and humane by comparison. He was wounded and decorated for his bravery by Germany.

As soon as his age permitted, my cousin enlisted in the British army. At the end of the war, he was able to deliver to the British the names of some Nazi criminals from his home province, none of whom "knew anything about atrocities" and none of whom "had done anything wrong." His parents perished in death camps.

From 1940 on, having left England for Palestine, I was able to communicate with my parents a few times via their friends in Sweden.

In Jerusalem, while attending the Hebrew University and preparing for exams licensing me as an English teacher, I tried to obtain a full-time position. I found myself competing with applicants endowed with the highest qualifications from English and German universities. In time I honed my knowledge and skills and became a tenured high-school teacher in Tel Aviv, conducting finishing classes for the official matriculation examinations, for which I published one of the first workbooks.

Around mid-1940 my parents informed me via Sweden that their U.S. waiting number had been called. I immediately sent their aged cousin in New York whatever modest means I could, knowing that the affidavit, based on financial support, at that time the *conditio sine qua non*, was likely to create a problem. I later learned that the said relative had just undergone major surgery which left her crippled, leaving my parents trapped in wartime Germany. Thus all my efforts proved useless.

In early 1941 my father died, mercifully, in his sleep. My frantic attempts to obtain my mother's temporary admission to Cuba were futile. In late November 1941 I received a Red Cross letter from my relatives who had fled from Alsfeld to the City of Essen, soon to be deported themselves, saying: "Mother resettled in Litzmannstadt-Ghetto, Pedlars Lane 17. Mother healthy. We all healthy."

Although I had been told by a well-informed English

lady that the fate of the European Jews was now hopeless, I had refused to believe it. I spent that afternoon running to the Red Cross Center, then to the depot for Care packages, and I spent most of the night worrying if there was anything that I could do from enemy territory to save my mother.

The next day was the only one in the half-century of my teaching career on which I was totally unprepared for my classes. It was also the only position in my life that I ever lost. As fate would have it, an almighty inspector came to visit our classes, including mine, which, I am sure, must have been rather dull. Of course, I should have explained the reason to the principal and written a letter to the inspector. But not knowing how important that one visitation might be, being very young und unused to defending myself, I did nothing. I lost that job, and along with it, my residence in the excellent mountain climate in Jerusalem, and my new friends.

I am sure that the Care packages, which I desperately sent my mother to Litzmannstadt (or Lodz) via the Red Cross, never reached her. From two survivors, one a former Lodz Kapo and another a pre-teenage boy at the time, I later found out some details about that ghetto and about my mother's fate. Those who were able to use four or five old sewing machines for piecework delivered to the German armies were entitled to daily "rations" of a little bread, a potato, often rotten and sometimes stolen, and some margarine. They even had a makeshift form of sparsely attended Sabbath services. My mother, being good at sewing, was still alive in March 1942, when she was called to appear before the *Judenrat* (Jewish Council) and interrogated about certain business debts owed my father by a number of Aryan customers, which the German Government decided to collect as part of the war effort. One month later, in April 1942, my mother, along with many others, was allegedly transferred to the gas chambers of Auschwitz.[1]

This information was obtained from a surviving Jewish Kapo, a former resident in my hometown of Trier. The report contradicts Rudolf Höss's memoirs in *Death Dealer*, which states, "The first transport from Lodz Ghetto arrived in Auschwitz on August 15, 1944."[2] From a surviving inmate, the only one of a family of five, I learned that innumerable victims of that incredibly overcrowded ghetto were often loaded on buses and driven to forests, where they were massacred. Whether the said Kapo, whose husband and one of her two sons were also murdered, misinformed us inadvertently, I shall never know. Nor shall I be able to find out if any small part of the Care packages, which, hoping against all hope, I sent my mother from Jerusalem, ever reached her or benefitted only the SS guards or the Jewish Council of that ghetto. Neither that Kapo nor the Jewish Council members could be consulted later—they are long deceased. In late 1944 the Lodz Ghetto was liquidated.

Did the prisoners, who were forbidden to talk, have any knowledge of what went on at the front? Snippets of information leaked through by the constant influx of new arrivals. What made some inmates of the innumerable death camps and ghettos cling to life? One was that America, the great hope, had entered the war. Rumors were also whispered that there were problems at the Russian front. There were even some covert contacts with Jewish partisan heroes, who had to brave the fourfold deadly enemies of starvation, exposure to freezing weather conditions, hungry wolves in the forests, and, first and foremost, Nazi spies and their collaborators.

Like my mother—my grandmother, uncles, aunts, and cousins were packed into boxcars and murdered in various death camps. One cousin, a tall, blond beauty, had a baby shortly before deportation. The bloodcurdling way in which the baby was killed before the parents' eyes, according to eyewitnesses, does not bear repeating.

In the early 1940s I also heard that a friend of mine, a medical student, who had followed her fiancé to South Africa, had died, allegedly of pneumonia.

Another shocking, mysterious death occurred in New York City in the 1950s. One weekend I interrupted my studies at Temple University and accepted an invitation of a former classmate from Würzburg, a pretty, intelligent woman in her late thirties, with the same quick, warm smile which I remembered from her youth. She seemed well adjusted with her husband and two lovely children. Despite our different routines, we maintained some contact. Later I heard that one day, without warning symptoms, she had jumped from the roof of their apartment building, a Manhattan skyscraper, to her death. No one has ever been able to find an explanation for this desperate act! Her parents had been deported and murdered.

I have heard people ask, "Why didn't they fight in the concentration camps? They were so many." A lot of the younger set did fight, knowing they would die anyway.[3] But how could the sick, starved, dying masses fight the machine guns and killer dogs of those countless mass murderers, to whom human beings were nothing but vermin—heinous criminals who were seen to shed tears when their dogs died?!

DÜSSELDORF EPILOGUE

The November 1938 pogrom in Germany, planned for some time and occasioned by Herschel Grünspan's shooting death of the ambassadorial secretary Ernst vom Rath in Paris (aimed at the ambassador himself), took on especially brutal dimensions in vom Rath's native city of Düsseldorf. Some printed records of the city, revealing details about the events before, during, and after the war, are useful in supplementing our knowledge gained by personal contacts. From the former principal of the Jewish School in Düsseldorf as well as his wife and several surviving faculty members and students, I learned about the fate of that once-elegant center of art and industries. An essay issued in Himmelgeist, a suburb of the city, on the occasion of the 1988 centennial celebration, includes the proud history of the Jewish population up to the moment of the total slaughter.

Before Hitler's takeover, Jewish citizens, being entitled to equal rights and completely emancipated, were patriotic, active participants in the cultural, political, and industrial life of this flourishing city and considered themselves, like in other German cities, "German citizens of Jewish faith."

Toward the end of the nineteenth century, organizations sprang up in some cities which questioned the integration, emancipation, and equal rights of the Jews. For example, when in the spring of 1888 a monument was to be erected, dedicated to the famous Düsseldorf-born poet Heinrich Heine (who had fled, under anti-Semitic pressure, to spend many years of his life in Paris), ugly flyers and brochures were circulated in opposition to building a memorial honoring "that talmudic Jewish swine."

Meanwhile, like the Protestant minority amid the growing Catholic majority of the Düsseldorf citizenry, the Jewish population was growing, too. In 1904 a synagogue was built with 1,700 seats, which soon proved much too small. The inauguration was performed, with a golden key to the city, under the auspices of the mayor himself. The synagogue was destroyed by the city administration exactly thirty-four years later!

Between November 9 and 11, 1938, four hundred synagogues and many more small prayer centers were destroyed in Germany, as well as innumerable dwellings and business places. It later became known that the Nazis had intended to accelerate drastically the expulsion of the Jews. According to statistics, as many Jews fled from Germany in the nine months between the *Kristallnacht* and the outbreak of the war as in all the previous six years.

During the *Kristallnacht*, seven Jews were murdered in Düsseldorf, seventy gravely injured, and the rest of the men transported to Dachau. Altogether 30,000 German Jews were shipped to concentration camps or "Kolas" (*Kon*zentrations*lager*, for short) during the *Kristallnacht*. Originally, wealthy Düsseldorf Jewish men aged sixteen to fifty were ordered to be arrested, but that limitation was not adhered to. Due to organizational problems, those who were not permanently disabled during their imprisonment were returned home in order to hasten their emigration and the aryanization of whatever business they still owned. The burning synagogues were not to be interfered with; only the fires which had spread to neighboring Aryan buildings were sprinkled with extinguishers. Eyewitnesses reported later that most of those watching the burning synagogues and prayer centers were silent and perhaps disapproving, whereas greed and jealousy prompted many onlookers to cheer at the destruction of the status symbols of wealth—oil paintings, candelabras, valuable antiques, cut-up Persian carpets, grand pianos. Photographs and any newspaper releases of those government-ordered destructive measures were strictly forbidden.

For esthetic and safety reasons, the smoldering synagogue and prayer centers (which were declared eyesores) had to be torn down after the fire. The Jewish congregation was ordered by the municipality to pay 20,500 Reichsmark for the damage caused by the Germans no later than November 25. The men still being in concentration camps, and such a large sum not being available anyway, the representatives of the congregation offered to sell the lot of the synagogue worth 360,000 Reichsmark to the city (the building was worth 800,000 Reichsmark before the fire). After countless farcical "negotiations" about phony "overhead costs," "soaring expenses," and others added, the municipal chicanery and theft ended with the city being the owner of the parcel.

In 1933 the Jewish congregation of the city counted 5,600 members. At the outbreak of the war there were still about 1,800 Jews in Düsseldorf. One building still owned by the congregation was used for religious services on High Holidays, as a school for the remaining children, for language courses preparing some desperate, still hopeful people for a start in emigration countries, and for rare events which the Jewish Culture Bund could still organize.

The cellar served as the only air-raid shelter for all the Jews. When the head of the congregation asked the city council for permission to add a protective wall, the letter in answer to the petition, discovered years later, displayed a heavy blue line drawn through the words "Jewish Congregation," followed by a scribbled note "This thing still exists??!!" ("Sowas gibt's noch??!!") It was the amazed, outraged response by a typical German who found the total Jewish annihilation process too slow.

The outbreak of the war practically meant the end of any hope for escape for most Jews still trapped in Germany. An official law against emigration was decreed in October of 1941. In February 1942 the last transport of eighty-one old, helpless people was shipped to Theresienstadt, and from there, those still alive were deported to their final slaughter.

Of four hundred students enrolled in the Jewish School in 1936, there were sixty-six left in October 1939. Until June 1942, a grotesque law required Jewish children to go to school, long after the last children had been packed onto cattle trucks rolling eastward.

According to reports released many years later, more than 2,000 Düsseldorf Jews were murdered between the *Kristallnacht* and the end of World War II.[4] An official report dated November 12, 1938, stated that during the *Kristallnacht*, 400 German synagogues were burned down, 76 more were demolished, 7,500 shops destroyed. The Jews were ordered to pay one milliard (a thousand million or one billion) Reichsmark to the German Reich.[5]

FOUR
IN VICHY FRANCE

Shortly after the outbreak of the war, my sister, like most residents of Strasbourg and the Vosges area, had fled southwestward from the eastern border to the inner part of France, which, after the German invasion, established a separate government with its seat in Vichy. Paradoxically, her typically German Marlene Dietrich looks got her into trouble: Under suspicion of being a German spy, she was detained for a few days in southern France until her fiancé in his army uniform rescued her and they got married.

My brother-in-law, also Jewish and German-born, had graduated from Strasbourg University and, like other refugees in France and England, immediately enlisted in the army. His German name was promptly replaced with a local one, as was also the custom in England. After the French capitulation in 1940 and the establishment of the Pétain government in Southern France, he received new official papers from the Vichy authorities. While the chances of amalgamating in the environment and surviving were better here than in the north, the Nazi conquerors and their henchmen were ubiquitous here, too, overtly and covertly, hunting down Jews and able-bodied non-Jewish men to be shipped to slave labor and death camps, sometimes via the transit camp at Gours.

One November afternoon, returning on his bike from a class he had given, to join my sister at their modest lodgings in a village near Clermont-Ferrand, he was stopped by a unit of SS men and ordered to stand in line along with dozens of other men. During the many hours they were kept standing in the rain, orders were constantly shouted in German while everyone was closely watched. He pretended not to understand a word, looking right and left to see what the others were doing. Being conscious of some telltale notes in his pockets, he slowly and carefully let them glide down inside his trousers and buried them very cautiously, unnoticeably scraping the muddy ground with his shoes. Everyone realized that asking for permission to step out of line in order to relieve himself would be tantamount to suicide, provoking severe injury by the SS.

He was hoping all the while that they would not order their captives to undress. For whereas circumcision was the law in France and had been for considerable time, the Nazis were experts at noticing the difference between the general French procedure and the Jewish ritual. The Gestapo and death-camp organizers were lawyers, doctors, engineers, and Ph.D.s, knowledgeable of minutiae related to "ethnic cleansing."

After many hours of standing at attention on that cold,

rainy November day, following screamed orders and being closely watched, Henri, my brother-in-law, along with a few others, was allowed to leave at night.

A few days later, riding on his bike, he passed a long line of men, among whom he recognized some Jewish acquaintances, mostly former classmates. They called him and urged him to join them waiting in line. They explained that the French government, in liaison with the German authorities, were offering to assist those Jews wishing to emigrate to South America in obtaining their documents—exit permits, passports, and visas. He saw the writing on the wall and suspected a trap. When he continued on his way, saying he would think about it, they called after him, "Mais vous avez tort!" ("But you are wrong!") Not one of that crowd was ever seen alive again.

Years later, rumors were heard that those hopeful young people had been transported to the east, where they perished, perhaps along with a large group of Jews who were driven into the swamps to drown.

My sister and Henri continued to live in their village as refugees from Strasbourg, raising chickens and vegetables, trying cautiously to find a way out via relatives in the United States or Palestine. Like some of their friends in France, they were able, though always fearful and often hungry, to survive the German occupation.

In 1945, very shortly after the official end of the war, my sister gave birth to their first baby, when there was a terrible food shortage in France, which, like all the countries invaded by the Nazis, had been drained of her resources—livestock, agricultural products, art, antiques. Unbelievably, the hospital could not provide any meals during her confinement, and her husband had to travel to and fro on his bike to bring her some food!

We were reunited for several weeks in the summer of 1947, when I visited them during my vacation, coming from the powderkeg of still British-ruled Palestine, just before the Marshall Aid brought relief to France and other European countries ravaged by Nazi aggression. This massive relief was the result of a law initiated by the American general and diplomat George Marshall, who insisted that a healthy Europe was the best guarantee to prevent World War III.

Instead of the booked and prepaid "direct" flight on an overseas British airplane, the trip from Tel Aviv to France on a four-seat small plane, which had to refuel every couple of hours, took one week along the North African countries, Corsica, and Switzerland and turned out to be far more adventurous than anticipated. Among many unpleasant surprises were the accommodations on stretchers in old roach-infested tents and barracks and the barely edible food "served" sometimes by German POWs, who, relying on our British/Palestinian passports, obviously assumed that we did not understand their curses!

FIVE

NAZI GERMANY FROM AN ARYAN PERSPECTIVE

Himmler's "Eugenic" Baby Factories

How was it possible that a modern democracy like Germany, famous for her most sophisticated technology and her sensitive, insightful works in the humanities, succumbed to the promises of a boisterous, screaming Austrian nobody, who turned the clock back to the Vikings of the darkest Middle Ages and brought about the most shameful and destructive period in the history of Germany and the rest of continental Europe?

Viewing the events in the Third Reich from the post–World War II perspective of "Aryans," full-fledged German citizens, many of whom lived outwardly unharmed through the twelve years of Hitler's "Thousand-Year Reich," is liable to create an ambiguous impression; those who cheered his inflammatory speeches and promises of glory most jubilantly were often heard to complain bitterly after

Part of this chapter was originally printed in *Jewish Currents* (November 1988): 36–38. It is used with the publisher's permission.

the war about their losses, suffering, and sacrifices and, overtly and covertly, to resent the postwar laws ordering the return of the stolen Jewish assets to the survivors or their descendents. A surprising number of Germans, Austrians, French, and others announced retroactively that they had been part of the "resistance movement." Even Pope Pius XII claimed that he, and Pope Pius XI before him, had been opposed to the Nazis' maltreatment, deportation, and murders of the Jews, while in fact both had lent deaf ears to any pleading to intervene on behalf of the victims, as the whole world knew; meanwhile the two popes praised Hitler's hostility against the Soviet Union.

Unbelievably, Pope John Paul II, in the name of the Vatican, is known to have announced considering Pope Pius XII to be elevated to sainthood! When we check the facts of his papacy, this sounds like a mockery![1] His predecessor, Pope Pius XI, also had done nothing to save the Jews; he sat on the throne of St. Peter disregarding the reports by his cardinals and other nobles of the church about the attacks and maltreatment of Jews, and he never excommunicated Hitler from the Catholic church.

His successor, before elected Pope Pius XII, at the time secretary of state of the Vatican, signed a concordat with Nazi Germany on July 20, 1933, which gave Hitler his first international success. He never condemned the Nazis for the mass murders of Jews all over Europe. Any official condemnation of his would have had an undeniable impact on Hitler and the world. Instead, he was known to have prayed, in 1941, for a quick German victory over Russia.

It is true that, around the turn of 1943–44, he went through the motions to rescue some Jews. But as is known, the majority of European Jews had been slaughtered by then. Besides, the war had already turned in favor of the allied forces.

Earlier, Pius XII had repeatedly expressed his opposition to Zionism and, in the name of all Catholics, to settling Jews in Palestine. He urged the world powers to find another territory for the Hebrews if they wanted a home. He warned against Palestine as a homeland for the "Hebrew race." He claimed that, while Palestine was once the homeland of the Jews, there was no axiom in history to show "the necessity of a people returning to a country they left nineteen centuries before." Catholics would object the world over. Besides, many Catholic lives would be endangered if he publicly blamed the Third Reich for its actions against the Jews, he maintained.

At the beginnings of the Nazi Party and its growth amid the economic and psychological depression of the German people during the late 1920s and early 1930s, the high-sounding promises and hate propaganda of the *Führer* and his military entourage were music to their ears.

As to their assurance "Today Germany, tomorrow the world," even some initial skeptics lulled their better judgement to sleep and abandoned themselves to their wishful thinking, to what Samuel Taylor Coleridge and later drama critics called "the willing suspension of disbelief." Powerful countries like England, with weak leadership at the helm, and the war-weary United States, in the grip of a recession, were duped, by Hitler's shrewd emphasis on his peaceful intentions, into a laissez-faire attitude until it was too late, disregarding the persistent, unpopular warnings of open-minded men like Winston Churchill.

The rapid change from a democracy to a totalitarian

government had been meticulously prepared for a decade or more by the NSDAP (the National-Socialist German Workers Party). Over many centuries of military tradition, the German population had been trained to follow the orders of the authorities. This partly explains the phenomenon of the tremendous power which Hitler gained at once, with his laws and lawlessness engulfing all strata of a nation "rich in military heroes, but . . . underdeveloped in civil courage," as Studs Terkel puts it.[2] The effects of the all-encompassing political, economical, social, and legal changes were swift. The Nazis knew well that fear is a powerful incentive. Opponents were silenced by the specter of "special treatment," that is, torture and execution, and by the impossibility of obtaining or holding a job without party membership. Store owners were won over by the sudden wealth obtained from the elimination of Jewish businesses, and those in the professions profited by their burgeoning practices after the dismissal of all the distinguished Jewish physicians, lawyers, accountants, and professors. Pragmatists, hedonists, released prison inmates, psychopaths, brainless and unprincipled creatures enthusiastically embraced the "new spirit," enjoying the windfall bestowed upon them from the stolen properties of the Jews and the overrun countries drained of their material and human resources. Then, during and after the collapse of the Reich, in keeping with the morals of Nazi mentality, some switched without qualms to sleeping with the enemy in exchange for some luxuries, while most of Germany and a large part of the rest of Europe lay in shambles.

Jews were treated as outlaws. The police had become lame ducks. They were replaced by the SA (the brownshirts), the SS and SD (*Schutz-Staffel* and *Sicherheits-dienst*, i.e., Security Service), the net of spies. The police were at best assigned to minor traffic violations. In any crime by the powers that be, they were conspicuously absent, following orders from above, like during the pogrom on November 9/10, 1938. Anyone who had a grudge, debt, or envy toward a Jewish person was free to denounce, assault, or eliminate him or her with impunity. My hardworking father, a World War I veteran like so many Jews, felt sure that the men with whom he had fought shoulder to shoulder for the fatherland would come to their senses. Stationed at the Serbian front, he had suffered a severe form of malaria. Another war veteran living in our city, who had survived World War I, but was wounded and lost his eyesight, was dragged to Auschwitz and lost his life in the gas chambers. My father never quite recovered from the assault by one of his debtors.

Some of the reports which one received from Germans about everyday life under Nazi rule have to be taken with a few grains of salt due to memory lapses, lingering party loyalty, and intentional understatements, or, in some cases, fear of retribution. The author Bernt Engelmann, who was a child at the time of Hitler's takeover, informs his readers that he had to rely heavily on the reports of others whom he interviewed as an adult. This may explain his far-too-euphemistic historic overview. Engelmann's information that, notwithstanding his half-Jewish ancestry and his and his parents' former membership in leftist organizations, he was put in charge of high-priority, top-secret activities behind the front lines seems too good to be true to the informed reader.[3] I have met only three half-Jews who escaped hell in Hitler's Germany; they were hiding or at least kept a very low profile.

The Nazis had spies everywhere and searched the records strenuously for part-Jewish ancestors and for underground or past leftist affiliations. They used brutal medieval torture methods to make people talk and reveal the names and locations of Aryan transgressors hiding non-Aryans or dissidents; and the rewards for informants were generous. Very few Germans risked their lives to hide any Jew(s), except some who did so for large sums of money.

Whereas, in their loyalty to Jews, old friends and neighbors were few and far between in Germany, the rancor and hatred of some populations toward the conqueror in the invaded countries resulted sometimes in taking sides with their Jewish residents, such as Denmark, Sweden, the three Beneluxe nations, and even Italy. In Germany there were a few exceptions who launched a coup d'état but failed, like the handful of idealistic students in Munich, who ended up on the gallows; and a group of generals, opposing the raving mad *Führer*, drunken with his vision of his invincibility and the worthlessness of human lives, who, rarely emerging from his bunker, insisted on the slaughter of their armies in the fierce, fruitless battle against Russia; they failed in their assassination attempt against Hitler and, of course, also paid with their lives.

Many non-Jews, too, were under constant surveillance. Trying to get even for a friction with a neighbor, one had only to denounce that person to the Gestapo. An incautious, secret complaint to a friend or even a family member about Goering's rearmament slogan "guns, not butter," swiftly and mysteriously got a "rumormonger" reported to the Gestapo. Listening devices planted in telephones submitted detailed knowledge to the net of spies about anyone listening at night to "nigger music" or "horror stories about Germany," and the Gestapo struck at the most unexpected moments.

An estimated 100,000 informants reporting to the SS, the Gestapo, and the SD, were everywhere. Any criticism was treated as treason. Anyone making a casual remark to those he trusted, who refused to be "gleichgeschalted" (mainstreamed or "brought into line") or who disobeyed any of the thousands of regulations and prohibitions, ended up in a concentration camp and was brought back to his family in an urn. Many hundreds even of Hitler's friends and helpmates, as well as his rivals among the high-ranking members of the SS and SA, who knew too much about his past and his private life, were dragged out of their beds in the middle of the night and driven to a place of execution, put up against a wall without explanation and shot. Sometimes it was just a case of mistaken identity of a similar-sounding name. Slavs, Jews, gypsies, handicapped persons, dissidents, religious leaders, and those under suspicion of being homosexuals were rounded up and dragged to concentration and slave-labor camps. Life was so cheap in the eyes of the master race, and for the hundreds of thousands immediately murdered or exploited to death, there was an ever-growing stream of millions to take their place. Meanwhile, many German officers and troops enjoyed themselves while stationed, or on furlough, in *Gaie Paris*.

The Nazis knew well the powerful incentive of fear, which they used effectively to smother any clandestine antigovernment attempt or any party member's plan to leave the country. I heard of one non-Jewish family planning to leave Germany, where the parents, after secret preparations, anesthetized their son, a devout member of the Hitler Youth, to smuggle him across the border without his knowledge and consent.

In the bible of the Nazis, Hitler's *Mein Kampf*, he states in the chapter dealing with the Jews that, if they weren't there, he would have had to invent them (i.e., as a scapegoat to be blamed for any mistakes or mishaps in the country). During the early months of the Third Reich, a joke was circulated that "the Jews and the bicyclists are to blame for everything—unemployment, bad weather, etc." Someone asked, "Why the bicyclists?" The answer: "Why the Jews?!"

In our early childhood, when we visited our grandparents in the summer, we often met their next-door neighbor, an elderly Catholic widow, Mrs. W., who had no children, relatives, or other friends. She owned a similar home and garden as my grandparents. Almost every evening after supper, she came visiting to discuss the events and problems of the day with our grandparents, who were her lawyers, her accountants, her nutritionists, and indispensable friends. Naturally, Mrs. W. continued this friendship and custom after Hitler's takeover.

After some months, whether through their ubiquitous informants or their spy patrols, the SS discovered this unlawful friendship. One evening, when she was returning home, they were waiting for her and in unmistakable terms and motions (of hanging) threatened her about the consequences of further "treasonous" visits like these.

We later heard that she died not long after, alone, at home. Can one die of grief? I believe my father did when he realized, after many desperate attempts to escape "resettlement" by emigrating to America, that it was too late.

My parents had a different story to tell about their elderly Catholic landlady, the widow who owned the house where they had rented a nine-room apartment and a garden. Having been secretly an avowed anti-Nazi for years and on friendly terms with my parents, she unexpectedly turned about-face and became extremely hostile after the November 1938 pogrom. As soon as the SS had finished hacking all our furniture and contents thereof to pieces, she watched them leave and came running, screaming at my desperate parents that she wanted them out at once! Before finding other, much more modest accommodations, my parents rented half the apartment out, furnished, to a non-Jewish couple, with their Aryan name at the entrance, and the mezuzah removed from the doorpost. Needless to explain, for Jews to find another apartment presented a major problem, especially after November 1938. Between 1940 and early 1942 the German government "solved" that problem by deporting all the Jews. Communal houses, confiscated from Jewish owners, offered a temporary refuge.

The Germans, most of whom later pleaded ignorance about the fate of the deportees, knew as well as the rest of the world that all those scheduled to appear at the railroad stations at night for "resettlement" and loaded on cattle-trains were driven to their death.

Meticulous records were kept, some of them discovered after many years, about the ghastly, grisly details going on at the Nazi death factories. There were witnesses to tell about these atrocities among both the survivors and the guards. One can also find out particulars by touring the sites of Auschwitz and other former death camps. The tortures and vivisectional experiments inflicted on prisoners by the perverts, serving no purpose, were praised and encouraged by Reichsführer Himmler as "valuable experiments on those who deserve only to die." Sadistic methods of slow death and maximally painful suffering were performed on those still in good enough shape to "qualify," like Russian POWs and other recent arrivals. Fellow prisoners were forced to carry out these diabolical tasks, used as predators against each other.[4]

In the late 1930s, and especially starting in World War II, Hitler announced the authorization of a euthanasia program, "Operation T-4," whereby "useless," mentally or physically disabled persons were to be liquidated. Two hundred thousand retarded and physically handicapped victims were secretly exterminated at night in an asylum in southwest Germany. Nearby residents seemed to know that those of them in fairly good physical condition were used as guinea pigs for medical experiments and then killed, while others were murdered outright. In 1941, when these murders became known, both the public and the church protested; but the secret nightly murders of public wards as well as paying inmates of asylums presumably went on.

The counterpart of the mass murders of crippled, disabled, unwanted, undesirable, or otherwise dispensable individuals was the introduction of factories programmed for systematic breeding of perfect Aryan specimens.

"FOUNTAIN OF LIFE": THE ARYAN BABY FACTORIES

Heinrich Himmler, one of the most powerful Nazi leaders, was the main creator of ten or more German baby factories dealing with the eugenics project of "*Lebensborn*." These factories were aiming at "Nordicizing" the nation by the mass production of "noble Aryans." Their objective was to serve as the nursery garden for Germanic blood, where a new superman type would be bred. Racially "flawless" big blonde underage girls, who fulfilled this noble duty, could choose whether to keep their babies or give them to the *Lebensborn* for adoption. The fathers of these born-out-of-wedlock babies were high-ranking SS members, whose names were kept secret, but were recorded in the autonomous registry of the particular home for racial qualifications. Funding was provided from confiscated Jewish holdings and from payments imposed on Jews to repair the damage of the *Kristallnacht* or to pay a tax for permission to leave the country for emigration. Hitler (who had refused to shake the hand of Jesse Owens, the outstanding African American track star and winner of four gold medals at the 1936 Olympic Games in Berlin) was quoted to have repeatedly expressed a wish for a Greater Germany with a population resembling "England's handsome sons," whom he would prefer not to kill in a war.

Sixteen- to eighteen-year-old girls of good Aryan blood were encouraged to come to the homes and bear as many children as possible. The war had left Germany with more women than men, but every woman was honor-bound to become a mother as often as possible as a service to the fatherland. One high-ranking officer, SS *Oberführer* Dr. Gregor Ebner, predicted that, thanks to *Lebensborn*, in thirty years Germany would have six hundred more regiments. If a woman was no longer able to continue bearing children—preferably at the rate of a child a year—she would sometimes be allowed to stay on and work in the home.[5]

One study written for Himmler entitled "The SS for Greater Germany—with Sword and Cradle" states that, after the conquest of Denmark and Norway, the Reich Commissioner's Department would assume all costs incurred by mother and child in the prospective baby factories of these two countries. *Lebensborn* homes sprang up also in several other countries—Poland, Luxemburg, the Baltic Region, the Ukraine, Yugoslavia, Rumania, and Czechoslovakia, where the SS were looking for children with physical features suggestive of Aryan blood. Many thousands of children were slaughtered in the conquered countries, except here and there a few because they were blond.[6]

What was the outcome of Himmler's massive pseudo-scientific genetic experiment? Research done in the 1970s revealed no appreciable difference in shape and coloring between the *Lebensborn* offspring and others. Some *Lebensborn* products were very tall, like a certain middle-aged, blue-eyed giant, who was the tour guide on one of my overseas trips. He never ceased to mention his attachment to his mother and his birthplace near Munich and evaded any answer when asked about his father. He did not realize that some elderly men in our group had participated in the Allied invasion of Germany in 1945 and were very familiar with the names, layout, locations, and purpose of the baby farms. After a few amicable questions, they felt sure about his origin.

After the capitulation and moral collapse of the population, the Allied forces tried to reorganize whatever they could in postwar Germany—to feed the starving population, to have the guards clean up the countless concentration camps and bury the dead, and to stem the tide of epidemics. Many of the leading Nazis had already fled to safety, along with the loot which they had amassed.

As soon as the shock about the massive destruction and the many millions of murders committed by the Nazis was over, the Germans allowed their recent past to sink quickly into oblivion. Compassion fatigue soon gave way to the general pride in the *"Wirtschaftswunder,"* the miraculous economic recovery triggered by the generous American Marshall Aid. When, during a fellowship at Princeton University in 1963, I asked a German history professor about his and his friends' attitude during the Third Reich and at present, he said, "I am a pragmatist. I did what was expedient for my son and myself. As for now, people want to forget. It is not considered refined to talk about these things in good company."

Talking to other Germans, I heard a number of euphemistic remarks about wartime attempts by some of their fellow countrymen to "save refugees," the "small percentage" of loyal Nazi supporters among the young, the "ambulances" and "police cars" after the *Kristallnacht* in Düsseldorf (I did not see *one!*), some SS wardens' "fear" of their prisoners' later reprisals. Hardly anyone mentioned the events before and shortly after Hitler's takeover—the crimes and corruption, the psychosis and mass hysteria of the cheering, spellbound crowds. "Forget the past, only the future counts," was the postwar slogan, when all Germans dreamed of a healed world.

One vacationing Bavarian elderly couple, whom I met in 1996, bitterly complained—totally ignoring all historical and chronological data—about the devastation which the Allies had caused in the German cities during the last phase of World War II!

SIX

LIFE AT AUSCHWITZ

When the Auschwitz camp was first opened in June of 1940, 728 Poles were admitted. In the initial stages, the prisoners were registered, issued some clothes and even underwear, usually dirty and either too large or too small, and told that there was no other exit from the camp except through the crematorium chimney. They were then driven to their "living quarters."

In the different phases of Auschwitz and other camps, as thousands of victims arrived daily, the accommodations varied, but they were always disastrous. Shortly after the opening of the camp site, the prisoners slept on straw put on the floor, still visible in one of the preserved buildings. Later there were pallets, sacks filled with straw, put on the floor at night and stacked away during the daytime. Blankets were issued, usually one for two persons. In a room for barely forty persons, two hundred had to sleep, and three or four had to lie on one pallet. Anyone who had to go out and use the latrine at night usually found his place on the sack taken. For most prisoners, sleep was impossible in these conditions; it was just a continuation of the day's suffering. In other concentration and slave-labor camps and quarries, the prisoners often had to lie on the floor or benches near the workplace at night.

As the crowds—along with the loot—increased and more and more workers were needed, albeit constantly replaced by new arrivals, the army of SS had to find a "solution" for the nightly placements. They introduced three-tier bunks in both the men's and the women's quarters. Each of the bunk beds, which took up the space of the whole room, had to be shared by two or three people. Each barrack or "block" had three storeys of bunk beds. Seven hundred to eight hundred persons were assigned to each block. But when a large transport arrived, the number was doubled in one block, and the prisoners were often moved to the cellars or garrets. At Birkenau the quarters were even more cramped. The camps had two types of blocks: wooden ones, actually horse stables, meant for fifty-two horses each, and others made of bricks. The number of men or women assigned to a block soon grew to a thousand.

Each block, filled to more than capacity with three, later four rows of bunks and berths, was damp and cold in every season, and the stoves running along the walls failed to keep it warm. The slimy mire between the aisles, the rotten straw mixed with mud, taken from the thatched roofs of nearby torn-down farm houses, along with hunger and thirst and the stench, drove away sleep. The middle and lower berths had no straw. Litters of rotten straw, mud, and dust were constantly falling from the top tier onto the lower berths. The occupants tried to cover their heads with whatever clothes they had. The upper berths were much in demand and quickly taken. If a prisoner of that space got up at night, he found it taken upon his return. For pillows they used their clogs and caps.

Those of the so-called inmates' self-government and others with special skills and important work assignments were given a bed each toward the turn of 1943–44.

The wooden clogs used as shoes hurt the prisoners' feet. Many had no footwear at all and cut their feet on the rocks and cobblestones covered with mud. The tiniest cut, injury, or infection festered and escalated into a life-threatening wound. The filthy, overcrowded situation, along with the starvation, made it impossible for any one to stay healthy for long. On the verge of despair, the will to live deteriorated along with, and sometimes before, the physical breakdown, as was evidenced by the number of corpses of those who had "run into the wires" and had to be removed daily. Sometimes they were shot by the guards before they reached the dense net of electrified wires surrounding the camps.

Once some inmates who had no footwear asked a Kapo for shoes or clogs, who submitted the need to his superior. One high-ranking SS officer responded by ordering the commandants of several concentration camps that the appropriate action, instead of pitying the "poor guys," would be to teach them, by flogging or the like, how to take care of their things.

There were also those who were deported late in the war from some Eastern European countries. Being confined in the inferno for a few months naturally offered a better chance of survival than being detained for years, that is, from the beginning or the middle of the war.

Clothes were never changed or laundered. Getting sick, being too weak and unable to appear at the roll calls, seeking help at the hospital, usually meant transfer to the gas chambers. Typhoid and dysentery were the most frequent epidemics. The hospital, too, suffered from bad sanitary conditions and lack of drugs and equipment. The water was contaminated and "not fit even for gargling," according to one doctor's statement.[1] The SS doctors made regular selections for eliminations among the multitude of sick patients the same way as among the so-called healthy ones, except that the sick had hardly any chance to be spared, unless for an unusual, badly needed skill.

Thousands of healthy prisoners, with the help of many medical assistants, were also chosen daily to be sterilized. Other surgical operations were undertaken to have medical students or assistants learn surgical procedures by performing them on living bodies, usually Slavic POWs. The experiments mostly ended with the prisoners' death.

At times, the SS men entertained themselves in the selection hunt and exhibited a strange sense of humor. On one occasion in early 1944, they drove a large number of victims, clad in drawers only, who had been selected by a doctor for extermination, out of the barrack. First, they were beaten and kicked. Then some were told to kneel down, and the SS put revolvers to their heads. They next ordered them to get up and run, and they shot them in the back.[2]

A gigantic administrative apparatus supervised the prisoners day and night. In the vast two independent

Auschwitz camps, Birkenau, and approximately forty sub-camps located mainly in Silesia, there were different sections of officers and their staff, all members of the SS. There were a managerial, a political, and an employment section, the administrative offices, and the hospital staff. Other SS officers, from their houses and grounds on the outskirts of the camp sites, also were alert and kept watch to prevent the escape of any inmate, as well as attempted petty theft or a suspicious move.

An enormous net of the prisoners' self-government extended the huge body of the SS. That self-government consisted at first exclusively of professional criminals, who were entrusted with watching prisoners at work, and another section while they were off work. At the head of the latter was the camp senior (*"Lagerältester"*) and his innumerable subordinates: the block seniors, warders and their substitutes, the room seniors, clerks, and Kapos. They all wore special armbands denoting their functions.

During the daytime, the hierarchy consisted mainly of the block seniors, who counted the prisoners during the roll calls and gave their numbers to the next higher ones in line, the SS block leaders, who verified the numbers and reported them to the "Rapport leaders," noncommissioned officers. The numbers were then collected and submitted to the senior officers or their substitutes. In the early stages, the last officer entered the figures in the "Book of Death." Later, this record was discontinued.

From the SS captains' and commandants' diaries, memoirs, notes, and speeches, details of the extermination process became known. It was the task of the "special detachments" of prisoners to maintain an atmosphere of the greatest possible calm by deceiving the victims, men and women separately, in their own language about their fate, of which the masses of new arrivals were sometimes unaware. Many women, after undressing, hid their babies among the piles of clothing.

According to one report of August 1942, the gassing procedure malfunctioned. Seven or eight hundred people were pushed into a space of ninety-three square meters and the door locked. The diesel motor wouldn't start! After three hours, the engine started at last. After thirty-two more minutes, the door was opened. All were dead. Twenty workers checked the mouths, which they opened with iron hooks. Dentists knocked out bridges, crowns, and gold teeth with hammers. The SS captain in charge proudly displayed the amount of gold in a large jar filled with teeth.

Later, prisoners were also gassed in special motor cars during the travels.[3]

An SS captain once overheard a conversation of three camp commandants about the number of Jews gassed at Treblinka, Belzec, and Sobibor. The latter, with about 350,000, came in last in the competition, about which they all expressed their regret.[4]

SEVEN

THE LOOT

A t a moment's notice, people of the invaded countries—Jews, priests, gypsies, POWs, leftist party members, Slavs, cripples, retarded persons—were rounded up and deported and sometimes mass murdered close to home. Many of these victims had valuables on their persons or in their little suitcases. Upon arrival at the camp, all had to undress and pass naked before the eyes of an SS doctor, who decided on their physical fitness. Whether considered capable of employment—usually an average of 25 to 30 percent (only 15 percent from some countries like Greece)—or driven immediately to be gassed, they all had to drop their belongings.

Staff members were always eager to participate in the selection operations, which often took place in the middle of the night, and which involved extra bonuses: one-fifth of a liter of Vodka, five cigarettes, and one hundred grams of sausage.[1]

The stolen properties left behind by the millions of victims were shipped to various concentration camps, notably to Auschwitz or its subcamps. It was a gargantuan task to sort the vast quantities of jewelry, clothes, and currency, which were stored in newly built and constantly added huts and sheds. The numbers of prisoners employed to sort day and night was constantly stepped up. Despite increasing pressure, the enormous SS and their staff of prisoners could not cope with the incredible wealth from most European countries anymore, and the piles of unsorted luggage and boxes went on mounting.

After the initial stages, any registration in Auschwitz beyond the tattooed numbers ceased; numbers were no longer sewn on prison clothes, along with the initial of the country and the triangle whose color indicated the reason for the confinement; and the labels bearing the name and address, and personal documents attached to the properties, were destroyed.

The stolen objects—valuables, eyeglasses, watches, clothing, bedding, furniture, and so on—were not limited to Auschwitz and its Silesian border camps alone. In only *one* of the reports from the Lublin camp, the legendary value was given as amounting to approximately 180 million Reichsmark.[2]

Besides, gold and platinum teeth and bridges extracted from corpses' jaws were melted into ingots and sent to the Sanitary Head Office of the SS.

The rest of the loot was sent to various Nazi posts along with lists, for which the cryptogram "*Aktion Reinhard*" was used. Many details were revealed in the records at the Millitary Tribunal in Nuremberg, based on documents from the WVHA-SS (*Wirtschafts-Verwaltungs-*

Hauptamt: Economic Administration-Head Office). Different articles were to be sent to certain assigned offices, about ten or twelve in all: watches, towels, tablecloths to the armed forces; eyeglasses to the Sanitary Office; articles of everyday use, like towels, suitcases, backpacks, to a department for enhancing Germanization called the "*Volksdeutsche Mittelstelle*." Furs went to Ravensbrück, clothes to the Ministry of Finances. A secret letter of 1942 from Himmler to one high-ranking commanding camp officer contained exact instructions about the kind and number of items from the Lublin and Auschwitz stores which were to be sent for Christmas to different groups of "*Volksdeutschen*," German-speaking residents in the annexed border countries, a total of about 250,000 pieces. They all were to receive a suit of clothes each, a hat, coat, three shirts, underwear, and other things for everyday use, along with a suitcase. Beds, blankets, and bedclothes should be provided to needy residents.[3]

The SS of the camp garrisons also benefitted by receiving articles from those killed in the gas chambers if they applied in writing. Their special wishes were usually granted. Many asked for baby carriages and outfits for infants.

Before the approach of the liberating allied forces in 1945, the Nazis hurriedly burned or otherwise destroyed whatever evidence they could and removed all valuables. The myriad items left on the museum sites were without financial value: small suitcases, faded clothes, spectacles, protheses, dishes, and large quantities of human hair, left over from those that had been used by tailors for warm lining. Postwar forensic analysis of the contents of huge bales revealed the origin of the material as human hair.

In Birkenau the Soviet army found six barracks, which the remnants of the retreating SS troops had set on fire, along with certain extermination devices. But they were only partly consumed by the flames. More than a million high-quality men's and women's clothes and shoes, suit-cases, articles of everyday use, and carpets had been spared by the flames. Among the names of some victims, which were still affixed to several articles, there were those of children, indicating age and other details, such as "orphan." However, other than the findings in those bar-racks, the names of the owners of all the loot and their per-sonal documents had been thoroughly destroyed.

EIGHT

SURVIVORS OF THE INFERNO TELL THEIR STORIES

How were the 1 percent of the many millions of prisoners able to stay alive and survive the unlivable and unsurvivable conditions in the countless extermination and slave-labor camps of the Nazis? Did it take youth, exceptional physical strength and health, unusual shrewdness and resourcefulness, a superabundant will to live, a badly needed work skill, strict obedience, or a bit of luck? Or perhaps a certain spiritual attitude and a character fabric providing the ability to disregard the total absence of everyday normal laws and the unspeakable suffering of others and oneself? Rumors of the United States having entered the war and of Nazi defeats on the Eastern front kindled a glimmer of new hope. Some of the stories which a few prisoners lived to tell are following.

TANIK

Tanik Z., born 1929 into a comfortable middle-class family in Lodz, Poland, was ten years old when the Germans invaded the country in 1939. Unlike the years of the gradually worsening situation for German and Austrian Jews, the Polish Jews were rounded up by the invaders at a few minutes' notice, and he, his parents, and his two sisters were arrested and locked up in the ghetto of the city, which the Germans renamed "Litzmannstadt." When his family members, along with many other Jewish residents of Lodz, were lined up for the Nazis' fateful "Right"/"Left" screams, his father told him, "Run, Tanik, run!" He did, trying to escape from the Germans, when he was stopped by a Jewish policeman, who grabbed him, saying, "If you run in the direction of that bridge, they'll shoot you. I shall smack you a few times, so the Germans will think that I am punishing you." That was how he was saved for the moment. That Jewish ghetto policeman took the child under his wing a few times.

One day in September of 1942, the Germans came into the ghetto and made a selection of the people whom they forced onto a truck for "resettlement," among them his mother and two sisters. The boy wanted to climb after them, but his mother prevented him, shouting, "Run home!" meaning the overcrowded ghetto room, which they had been sharing with twenty other persons. Once again, his life had been saved.

Soon after, the Germans rounded up the children. Tanik's father hid the boy in the usually locked basement, put leaves and debris over him and a metal sheet which he found, and more leaves. The Germans came to the basement entrance once or twice, shot off the lock, took a pitch fork and started moving it around in the leaves. The boy saw a German boot and was hit with the pitchfork, which was very painful, but he kept quiet. After a few more attempts to discover if anyone was hiding, the Germans left. His father had been taken away while he was hiding.

Conditions became quite unbearable. Being left all alone and starving, he tried to kill himself a few weeks later by jumping from the third floor, but was stopped by a man (another policeman), who took the child to stay with him in his crowded room from then on.

He learned to stand very straight at the roll calls in order to look taller and older than he was, and he lied when asked about work skills, pretending that he was a carpenter and a metal expert. For whatever little rations were distributed monthly to the working prisoners, each had to find a safe hiding place, otherwise they would be stolen, and complaining resulted in death. Knowing when the truck with potatoes usually arrived, he sometimes managed to use a long pole sharpened at the end to steal a potato, a practice which he continued when he was transported to Auschwitz in 1944. Some boys followed his example. When he saw that one of them was caught and executed, he discontinued stealing.

After two months at Auschwitz, he was forced on a cattle train and transported to a munitions factory near Gerlitz, where he worked along with two thousand other people. In the center of that camp, there was a shed with pigs and rabbits owned by the head of the camp. He managed a few times, while nobody was around, to steal some food from the pigsty, which was far better than that for the workers.

In early 1945 Tanik and other munition workers were taken on a death march, where most of them perished. One or two weeks later, Tanik, now fifteen, and the other survivors were returned to Gerlitz, where the factory had been almost completely destroyed by the Russians. The workers were forced to build antitank trenches. In early May of 1945, as the Russians were approaching Gerlitz, the camp director announced that, by an order from Berlin, the workers were all free.

Even now, with the victors surrounding Germany on all sides, any euphoria on the part of a prisoner still often meant death. In the pictures taken by the Allies or the Russians, some of the "victims" stand out by looking well fed, even overweight, in far too tight outfits. Some guards had the humorous idea of stripping the emaciated prisoners of their "uniforms," their striped pajamas, in order to escape arrest and punishment by posing as prisoners themselves. Resistance on the part of any weak, skeletal inmate resulted in a last-minute death.

Tanik, now almost sixteen, decided, like some other survivors, that as soon as he could stand straight, he would return to his former Polish residence before the German invasion, hoping to join his family.

Sam

In the spring of 1938, having graduated from the Jewish Teachers College in Würzburg, Sam obtained a one-room school position in a large city. The twenty-five Jewish students were aged six to fourteen. Sam was fond of children, and making the most of the different age groups, working with one section at a time while assigning reading, writing, or arithmetic tasks to the rest, was quite a challenge for a beginning teacher. He focussed all his energies on making his job a success, and he soon earned the respect and trust of his students and their parents. The demanding schedule of the sheltering Orthodox teachers college, remote from the disturbing political and racial realities, followed by his first teaching position, created in him a false sense of security about the future of the Jews in Germany and the rest of the European continent. Gradually, the enrolment in his school as well as in his synagogue decreased, as several children, along with their families, left Germany.

After the *Kristallnacht* of November 1938, Sam awakened to the brutal fact that his success at his beloved job was misleading him to neglecting his safety and his future. He was not a Zionist. But he had some distant relatives in the United States, and in 1939 he secured a waiting number for immigration—and he waited. Considerable time passed till his number was called. A detailed correspondence with his relatives followed. Then the United States entered the war, and suddenly it was too late.

In late 1942 he was officially notified of the day when he and his remaining fourteen students would be fetched at school for "resettlement," while his and their parents would be picked up at home. A note indicated the exact size and weight of the allowed small suitcase or backpack. At the scheduled time, no questions were asked, no tantrums by the children, who were clinging to their teacher. They were all loaded on cattle trains and transported to Auschwitz. None of the children survived.

Upon arrival, when the prisoners were asked about special skills and work experience, Sam reported that he was a teacher. He was short, not heavy, but healthy, and he was immediately assigned to forced labor. After about two weeks, a guard ordered him to report to the *Lagerführer*, the "*Herr Kommandant*" (head officer of the camp). He was briefly interviewed. Apparently he had been watched at work, and in the midst of his students when they were picked up for deportation. From then on he was teaching the head officer's six and another officer's four children, all of different ages—in short, a sort of a small one-room school situation. He taught them reading, writing, arithmetic, geography, and the older ones basic English, and he received better treatment and more food, while still assigned to a portion of forced labor. He was no taller than the youngest of his students; but the *Lagerführer* told the children in an unmistakable tone that any one of them who was inattentive, lazy, or disobedient would be punished by him personally.

Sam now had some hope that his skill and experience could save him, provided he kept his wits together, and the atrocities around him, about which he was powerless to do anything, did not make him lose his mind nor his pragmatic attitude; and, most important, he would not get hopelessly ill. Consulting the doctor or nurse for any ailment usually meant death.

Doctors (or medical students) and nurses were present at each of the hundreds of camps in Germany and the invaded countries, for the needs of the commanding officers and the prison guards, for reporting sick inmates, and for diagnosing epidemics. Members of the medical staff were given priority treatment. One pretty, fairly young blonde physician from Lodz, who had survived the ghetto and then Auschwitz with her husband, a former lawyer, had entrusted her baby, along with a substantial sum of money, to a gentile Polish couple (her former patients) after the German invasion. She told us that she had once even succeeded in leaving the ghetto to visit her baby. After World War II, the three of them, all apparently in pretty good health, came to Israel, where she was promptly appointed as the head physician of a small new medical branch, though subtropical diseases were, and probably always remained, a *tabula rasa* to her.

MIRAM

Miryam, aged fifteen at the time of the November 1938 pogrom, from an Orthodox family in a small town in Hessen, had her high-school education at a Jewish religious private school interrupted. She was deported with her parents to Theresienstadt in 1941, and from there to Auschwitz-Birkenau in 1942. She was immediately separated from her parents, not knowing what had become of them. Being strong and healthy, she was put to hard menial work. Later she sometimes received food from an SS man who liked her looks—no need to ask what this meant.

Despite her own exhausting, hopeless, inhuman situation, nothing around her escaped her notice, and being highly sensitive, she suffered not only from her own afflictions, but also from those of others around her. Unlike many other deeply religious persons, whose faith collapsed amid the horrors of the camp, she clung to her belief and convinced herself that God was there through all their suffering and that he, too, suffered along with the prisoners. Often, during her demeaning tasks, she remembered a passage from her Judaic studies, in which she had been steeped before her deportation. This gave her strength in her despair. Through pain, sickness, fear, starvation, filth, demoralization, during two and a half years of incarceration and the death march, she struggled intensely to hold on to her faith in God, which she never lost. Later, in the displaced persons (DP) camp, the flashbacks of her suffering found an outlet in amazing, exquisite therapeutic poetry. There were others, such as some gifted painters, who tried to escape from their haunted consciousness by finding release in sketching and painting.

Strong, healthy, attractive girls in their teens, and even in their preteens, were often used as prostitutes for young unmarried SS men. They received better rations and better, cleaner living quarters. Unless they perished in the death marches toward the end of the war, when many camps were liquidated, it was one way to survive. Nobody talked about this, but from certain remarks, sometimes much later, it was easy to figure out. Some got married in the DP camps, others after emigration to Israel or the United States. They usually settled down in a normal, occasionally even Orthodox lifestyle, had children, became devoted wives and mothers, and tried to forget past events, for which they were not to blame.

After World War II, among the new students in one of

My parents after their wedding, June 1913

My parents about 1933

My father as soldier, WWI

My National Political Training class at the Aryan School, January 1934. I am in the middle.

One of my classes in Tel Aviv with six teachers, including myself. The usual class size was fifty-five.

My sister and her husband, Henri, after their wedding, Vichy France

My sister, the perfect "Aryan" image

My sister, five months pregnant, and her husband, Vichy France, 1945

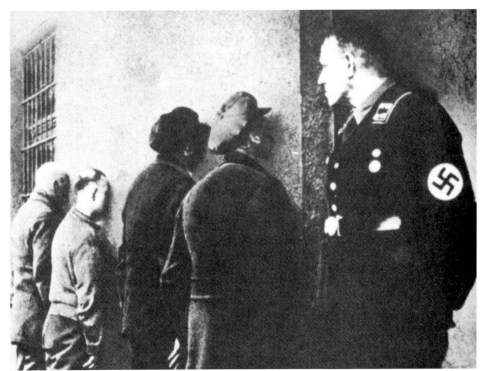

One of Himmler's dedicated officers lines up Polish civilians, probably on suspicion of being Jewish. Between them, Himmler's SS and Gestapo slaughtered 2.6 million of Poland's 3 million Jews. *(Courtesy of the Spring Valley Holocaust Museum and Study Center, provided to the center by YIVO Institute Photo Archives.)*

A civilian round-up from the Lodz ghetto, to be transported or killed. *(Courtesy of the Spring Valley Holocaust Museum and Study Center, provided to the center by YIVO Institute Photo Archives.)*

Early Nazism in practice. A round-up of actual and alleged Communists by the SA in 1933. (Courtesy of the Spring Valley Holocaust Museum and Study Center; provided to the center by YIVO Institute Photo Archives.)

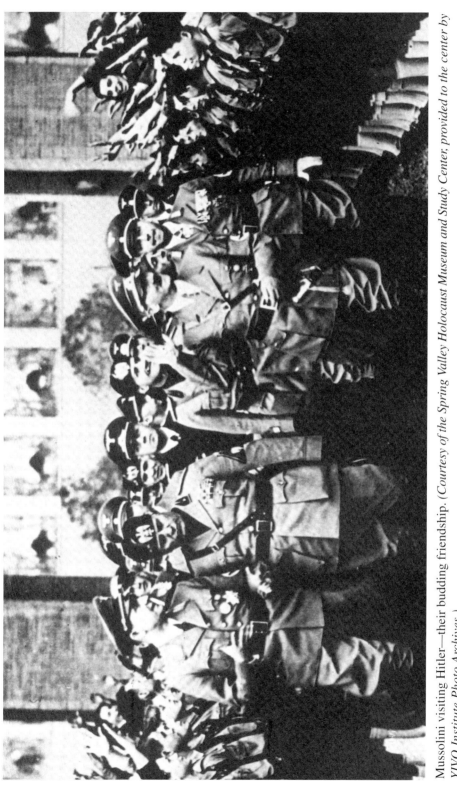

Mussolini visiting Hitler—their budding friendship. (Courtesy of the Spring Valley Holocaust Museum and Study Center; provided to the center by YIVO Institute Photo Archives.)

Midnight rally glorifying military might. (*Courtesy of the Spring Valley Holocaust Museum and Study Center, provided to the center by YIVO Institute Photo Archives.*)

Hitler touring Paris—his sole visit to the French capital. *(Courtesy of the Spring Valley Holocaust Museum and Study Center, provided to the center by YIVO Institute Photo Archives.)*

my Tel Aviv high-school classes, there was a quiet, intelligent boy, Polish-born, whose fate was known to our faculty. He had been imprisoned at Auschwitz with his father, each assigned to a different working squad. After careful preparations, his father planned their escape. At night, when they were fleeing, he first, his father following and shielding him with his body, his father was shot and fell, shouting to him to run. The boy was saved.

From survivors' reports; notes of the commanding head officer Rudolf Höss (the *Lagerkommandant*); tour guides' comments; a film; exploration and printed information on location—details about the goings-on at Auschwitz-Birkenau could be learned. Despite the strict secrecy enforced by the huge armies of SS and subordinate functionaries, often professional criminals, who supervised the prisoners day and night, and their feverish attempts to hide, burn, and otherwise destroy the evidence before the approaching conquering troops of the allies from the west and the Russians from the east, their atrocities, crimes, and inhumanity became known.

Glass jars buried by Polish and Austrian members of the Resistance movement were found later. Prisoners who were taken to work at the outskirts of the camp used a code by which to communicate with the outside world on tiny smuggled notes scribbled on cigarette paper, hidden in a pen, an apple, an old shoe-sole, a piece of garbage. The members met at places bearing large signs "Quarantined for Typhus," which the Nazis, afraid of contagion, avoided.[1]

Stores and trucks carrying food and other supplies for the prisoners were often rifled by the SS. Their wives took what they wanted and used flour, magarine, sugar, and potatoes, which were sent for the prisoners' rations, at their sumptuous parties for guests, among them Himmler and other high officers. They also sent parcels to their relatives in Germany. One prisoner employed in the residence of an SS officer described the affluence in that household as contrasted with the tragic sights of the sick, starving prisoners, many of whom were reduced to "stumbling corpses."[2]

But if a prisoner was reported to have stolen an apple, a piece of raw cabbage, or a dead man's shoes, he was executed. As we learned during the Eichmann trial in Jerusalem, one teenage boy, who stole an apple from a tree on the way to work, was forced to hang himself. To terrorize and weaken the prisoners, they were all ordered to watch the scene. When he was too weak to carry out the order, he was severely beaten and forced to try again until at last he succeeded!

Despite the danger, however, favorite inmates sometimes received bits of food from subordinates who had access to it.

In addition to the supplies for the prisoners, the SS had another source to enrich themselves, namely the delivery of inmates to be exploited for slave labor at the weapons, ammunition, and chemical factories of Krupp, I. G. Farben, and Union Werke, all of which paid the SS for the slaves' working hours.

One of the nightmares was the daily roll call protracted for many hours, separately for men and women, during which the prisoners were forced to stand at attention in rain, snow, or blazing sun with their heads uncovered. Originally there were three roll calls daily, one hour long each, which were reduced to twice a day before and after working hours. Even the strongest, like the Russian POWs, were too sick and exhausted to stand straight, and many had no shoes or coats. In the women's quarters at Birkenau, as time went on, most of the prisoners were barely covered with rags. Once a roll call lasted from 7:00 in the evening to 2:00 P.M. the next day, that is, nineteen hours. Anyone too sick and weak to stand at attention was severely beaten. Those who were dying of typhoid or dysentery were laid on the wet ground in the mud and later taken to the gas chambers.

Ethnic cleansing through extermination being the purpose of the innumerable death camps, thousands were killed daily at Auschwitz by being driven from the trains directly into the gas chambers, which, after the first slow, torturous experiments in September 1941, were perfected in late 1942 to function more efficiently and quickly by poisoning large masses of the people fed into them. Besides, there were also constant "selections" to be killed during roll calls or at night by shooting, hanging, or injections with poisonous chemicals.

As to those in the large work force, there were many "offenses" for which the penalty was death in various forms, graded in length and intensity of suffering. Not that the SS needed any justification for their murders and atrocities. But they did need huge numbers of slaves for the work. The "crimes" deserving deadly punishment ranged from using the latrines during working hours or roll calls, collapsing, or bartering a gold tooth for bread, to disobeying an order, trying to escape, being slandered or reported —usually without an investigation—as being or having been a member of the Communist Party or the Resistance, or as retaliation for working at the same squad and having failed to prevent or report an escape. Even without the gas chambers and crematoriums and the death penalties, the daily number of persons dying from starvation and diseases was enormous. Those not yet reduced to skeletons were also used to be experimented upon or sterilized by the many doctors at the Auschwitz-Birkenau camp.[3]

One frequent form of punishment was flogging. The prisoner was forbidden to moan or scream with the pain and had to count the lashes loudly in German. If he made a mistake, the lashes started anew. For sport, the SS sometimes added ten or twenty strokes to the usual twenty-five. The victim often lost consciousness during the procedure and usually died afterward as a result of festering boils and necrosis.

Another penalty was to be shipped to the Mauthausen quarries, where the survival rate was nil, or to continue work in off-hours at the hardest tasks under the supervision of the strongest and meanest Kapos, being frequently beaten. Most of them returned dead or half-dead at the end of the day from those penal assignments.

One slow and extremely painful punishment was hanging by having the wrists tied behind the lower back and then lifted to be hanged, so that the shoulder joints were yanked out by the body weight. The head and upper part of the body slumping down, the victim gradually suffocated.

For those who had tried to escape there were the "Dunkel-Zellen" ("dark-cells") and "Steh-Zellen" ("standing-cells"). During our group tour in 1990, these torture chambers were still preserved in all the diabolical details. The scratches of the desperate victims gasping for air were still visible on the heavy wooden doors.

In one "Dunkelzelle," up to thirty-eight prisoners were locked for several days without food and water in a small windowless room, with a heavy wooden door hermetically sealed, so that no air could penetrate. The oxygen was soon used up and the heat became unbearable. The stronger ones moved toward the door, trying in vain to scrape the door with their fingernails to get some air. The men took their clothes off and gradually died from heatstroke or asphyxiation. After several days, the door was opened and the naked bodies were removed. Once, after three days, one person survived to tell about it.

The "Steh-Zelle" was a cubicle with standing room for sixteen persons squeezed in an upright position against each other like sardines. In the evening, after work, without food or drink, the culprits were made to crawl through a narrow space at the bottom into that space—no room to sit—where they were standing all night, watched by German Kapos, who were smoking and talking, using up the last supply of air. In the morning, the men were ordered out through the crawl space and driven to work without food and drink again. Fasting and working all day, they were taken back into the "Steh-Zelle." This was repeated for several days until they collapsed from suffocation, starvation, and disease.

In late 1942 there was a mutiny and an escape planned at night in the women's quarters at Birkenau, led by some recently arrived French Jewesses. It was reported to Kommandant Höss, who immediately hurried to the scene with his SS men. The instigators were killed with axes and poles, some actually decapitated. Others were killed by injections. Ninety female prisoners were killed during the mutiny and many more in the aftermath. During the investigations following the attempt, many women were tortured by having their fingernails extracted, having needles inserted into particularly sensitive parts of their bodies, or having water poured down their throat causing suffocation, and they were constantly beaten. Those who survived the tortures were sent to penal companies (which was tantamount to death), or shot or hanged. None of the women betrayed anyone.[4]

One night, in August 1944, fierce resistance was offered by several thousand Gypsies, who were driven from their camp at Birkenau into the road by the SS and ordered to march to the crematorium. They disobeyed the order, tried to run away, and screamed at the top of their lungs, waking up everybody. In the morning, the Gypsy camp was empty and all was quiet.

Some of the Resistance fighters' activities were discovered and reported to the SS. By order of the Kommandant, the whole prison population had to watch their hanging. Already on the gallows, with the nooses round their necks, they shouted, in Polish or German, "Today we, tomorrow you!" "Death to Fascism!" "Long Live Poland!"

One of the many Jews in Palestine who volunteered to join the British forces during World War II was a young girl, a talented author and poet, Hannah Senesch. She asked to be trained as a parachutist. Her missions to land in European countries enabled her to contact several resistance groups. She was caught by the Germans, tortured, and made to confront her mother in a Hungarian concentration camp. She was executed at age twenty-three.

Even in the desperate conditions of the camps, a compassionate person was sometimes found who sacrificed some of his or her starvation ration, issued to those in the work details, to a sick inmate, perhaps just above the forbidden age of childhood, to prevent that fellow prisoner, too sick to stand straight during the headcount, from being "eliminated."

There were also some prisoners who would do anything for a morsel of food, some who collaborated with the Germans for a promotion, better rations, a chance to live another day. That was what the Nazis wanted—in the unbearable physical and emotional hardships, to use the prisoners as predators against their fellow inmates.

The question has often been asked: What was the permanent effect on the disposition and the frame of mind of those who survived that purgatory? Did soft-hearted, sensitive individuals become hardened, or selfish, callous characters turn compassionate? It seems that the basic *Weltanschauung*, the philosophy of life, of most survivors did not change essentially, nor did their psychological setup.

In the more than 1,000 concentration and extermination camps, more than 10 million perished; 4 million of those in Auschwitz-Birkenau, the largest camp.[5] Of the approximately 14,000 Soviet POWs at Auschwitz in September 1941, there were 92 left at the last roll call on January 17, 1945, shortly before the Russian army entered the camp.[6]

In front of the crematorium entrance, several gibbets are still visible today. Some of the criminals convicted at the Nuremberg trials were executed there. On one gallows, according to the record, the first camp commandant, Rudolph Höss, was hanged by the Poles on April 16, 1947.

NINE

AFTER THE LIBERATION

FREE AT LAST!!

It was not exactly the freedom most survivors had dreamed about. Especially those in the German DP camps and stranded all over Europe who were of Polish or Russian origin were closely watched in their movements. Most of the emaciated reminders of the German savagery, all of whom tried to recuperate a bit from the years of horrors, felt unwelcome. Worse—a group of former residents of the Polish town of Kielce, who had been in death camps, kept in hiding, or joined the underground, got organized, and in 1946, trying to locate some family members and perhaps to retrieve their properties, visited their Polish hometown, which had had a large Jewish congregation before World War II. The townspeople, living comfortably in the stolen homes, resented the unexpected return of the seventy-two Jews, and they killed seventy of them by stabbing, beating, or hacking them to pieces. This massacre was reported by eyewitnesses and became known as the "Kielce Pogrom."

Tanik, having strengthened a bit in a German DP camp, wanted first of all to find his family. In 1945 he escaped from the camp after a few months and made his way to their former residence in Lodz. He soon became convinced that no one of his family and his 128 relatives was alive. On his way back, he was arrested by the Germans and jailed for several weeks, after which he was sent back to Poland. At least he felt he was free now! He joined the underground, helping young people to enter Palestine illegally amid the threat of a new Holocaust, imposed by the British and the hostilities of the Arabs. He and many others who tried to enter Palestine, arriving on unseaworthy boats, were joined by many American Jews. All were arrested by the British and confined behind barbed wire in concentration camps on Cyprus or Mauritius. Tanik was incarcerated on Cyprus for nine months. The Americans had smuggled tens of thousands of refugees into Palestine between 1946 and 1948. World sympathy was at last on the side of the Jewish fighters, still weak from the years in concentration camps. The British, who had helped to free the slaves from Nazi concentration camps, now threatened a renewed Holocaust. They at last released the detainees under international pressure before giving up their mandate.[1]

Tanik joined a kibbutz near the Syrian border, where they were under constant attacks by the Syrians. In 1949 he was recruited in the Israeli army, where he served until 1953. He then became a driver and partner of the Egged Bus Company. In 1955 he met Rita, Russian-born, also a survivor, who had been four years old when the war broke out. Three months later, they were married, he twenty-six, she twenty. Soon after, his bus was attacked by some terrorists. Nine passengers were badly injured, but Tanik escaped unharmed.

In 1961 Tanik, Rita, and their two daughters emigrated to the United States, where he changed his name to Teddy. Life in this country has been good to them. But Teddy was carrying a heavy burden on his shoulder all the time. He could not find peace of mind because he had never been able to shed any light on the fate of his parents and sisters. In May of 1990 Teddy and Rita traveled to Poland in a desperate search for some clue about the death of Ted's family. After a lot of research and inquiries, following the route his family had taken during the last few days of their lives, they became convinced that his parents and sisters had been taken to the Chelmno death camp, where, according to some figures, 240,000 Jews and 20,000 non-Jews were gassed, burned, or shot. An engraved monument bears some record of the events. Chelmno, they found, is a beautiful area now, surrounded by lakes, trees, and flowers, without any resemblance to a former death camp. After more than half a century, Ted has now become quieter, having uncovered the fate of his family at last.

Like most other survivors, Sam, the teacher, was skin and bones after the liberation. Being alone, his parents murdered, along with the rest of his former congregation— as soon as he felt physically somewhat fit, he began to gather a group of surviving children in the camp and donated some of his time to help them absorb part of the education which they had missed. At the same time, he got busy locating the whereabouts of his cousin in the United

States, whom he then contacted. He eagerly worked on his emigration plan, for which he had so fatefully missed the deadline in 1941.

With the Nazi dictatorship ended, being German-born, he would have had no problem, once he had restored his health, to be reinstated in a teaching position. This was totally out of the question for him. He had no wish to fight his complete alienation from the "fatherland" and to make an attempt to readjust. Although he did survive, after what he had gone through and witnessed, he could not forgive and forget. He was only yearning to get out, start a new life far away, and leave it all behind.

In 1948 he was admitted to the United States, adjusted in time to make a living, got married, they had a son, and they gradually made some friends.

Miryam, aged twenty-two at the time of the liberation, sick and dangerously underweight, her parents, relatives, and friends dead, her schooling interrupted, but her keen intelligence and her sensitivity intact, remembered an uncle in New York City. With a little help, she located his address. While slowly getting better and putting on some weight, she found her own way to get over her gruesome recent years. While in the DP camp, she realized that she had to get on with her life. In the United States, she got married and had children and lived outwardly the life of a dutiful wife and mother. All the while, over several decades, she poured out her interior monologues about her spiritual struggle in the extermination camp in innumerable accomplished poems, which, if classifiable, can perhaps be categorized as expressionist. She never showed these pieces to anyone, nor did she offer them for publication. Most of them were found after her death in 1997. She never craved praise nor acknowledgment. While many other survivors of death camps, wars, and various dangers were hungry for beauty, prestige, success, wealth, possessions, she disregarded honors, niceties, finery, and entertainment. She raised her three children in the same uncompromising devotion to God's laws and Jewish rituals.

She later heard about the fate of a young classmate from a prominent, very devout family. He was the only member left behind in Holland after the rest of the family's emigration to the United States, and in 1943 he was deported to Auschwitz. Being deeply religious, and trusting a Higher Power more than the SS thugs around him, he secretly sought comfort sometimes in his accustomed daily prayers. This was noticed and reported to the SS. He was punished by dying in a particularly painful way, which haunted her long after the liberation.

Among those who were considered lucky to emigrate in early 1938 was the rabbi of the Trier congregation. He left Germany with his wife and their youngest son to join his daughter and her family in Holland. His two older sons had already been admitted to England, and another one to the United States. Before the advent of Hitler, his daughter, a pleasant young woman, had been somewhat active volunteering as a counselor for our group of early teenage girls. In a royally prearranged meeting in Marianske Lazne (Marienbad), she had been introduced to her future husband, a tall, dark, handsome, wealthy young man, and his family from Holland. It was a fairy-tale marriage, which all of us girls dreamed about.

On May 10, 1940, the Germans invaded Holland.

How they were all able to keep alive for three and a half years after the Nazi onslaught is not known. At the end of September 1943, the whole large family was deported to the Dutch transit camp of Westerbork, and a few months later to Theresienstadt; from there they were shipped to their death at Auschwitz.

One of the lucky boys to escape from Holland was saved from the Nazis' slaughter by his two devoted older sisters. When the invaders started arresting able-bodied boys and men for transports to slave-labor camps, they hid their brother in a cave, where he lived for many months. Every few nights they brought him food, blankets, and fresh clothes till he could board a Palestine-bound vessel. The three had fled to Holland, where no one knew that they were German Jews—no Christian looked more "Aryan."[2]

"Forget the past, live for the future!" was the guiding principle of the parents of my Jewish friends from Australia, whom I first met in the 1980s during my tour of Spain. The young couple was on an extended honeymoon trip around the world, she a recently graduated physician, he an accountant. They had rented out their house, a wedding gift from her parents, and they financed their mortgage payments and their frugal, adventurous global tour from the rental proceeds. Her Polish-born parents had met as DP's after having survived slave labor at different camps, regained some strength, and recuperated. They got married, and with the help of kind relatives, were admitted to Australia. There they set out to live a normal life as conservative Jews, determined to devote all their energies to their new life. First they had the tattooed numbers on their left forearms, which branded prisoners like cattle, surgically removed. They went into business and had two children. While they did not anxiously avoid any thought of the past, they did not indulge in it. His parents, too, were Holocaust survivors.

A few years later, I had a reunion with the young couple in their home near Melbourne, and I met the two additions to their family, a little boy and a baby girl. At the time she was mostly home with the children and worked a double shift as a doctor on Sundays, planning to add a third child.

Hearing all the gruesome and sometimes inspiring stories of suffering, bravery, and vitality, one is reminded of the arguments between two brilliant minds of the seventeenth and eighteenth centuries, respectively, namely the German philosopher Gottfried Wilhelm Leibnitz and the French author François Marie Arouet Voltaire. In the witty, on the surface bantering classic *Candide*, Leibnitz's optimistic theory that all human suffering and disaster is a necessary ingredient of a basically benevolent cosmic plan was exposed to ridicule by Voltaire. The French writer summed up his own cynical view of the savage world in this statement: "Les trois ingrédients les plus importants de ce bas-monde, ce sont la guerre, la famine, et la peste!" ("The three most important ingredients of the world are war, famine, and the plague!") One could argue that both theories are questionable in that human history moves perhaps in the direction of ancient Greek nature philosophy, which conceived the world order in terms of *panta re*, that is, a wavelike movement, in which harmful, turbulent epochs alternate with beneficial ones.

TEN

BETWEEN PALESTINE AND ISRAEL

As soon as World War II ended, the war in Palestine began.

For centuries, groups of persecuted Jews had fled from European countries and settled in the land of the Bible. In 1895 a handsome, tall, Hungarian-born Jewish reporter from Austria, Theodor Herzl, attended the trial in Paris of Captain Dreyfus, accused of treason. Deeply disturbed at the anti-Semitic screams of the crowd and convicted that the helpless Jewish officer was innocent and framed by his Christian fellow officers—the real culprits—he published a pamphlet, "*Der Judenstaat*" ("the Jewish State"), emphasizing the urgent need of a Jewish country, and he founded the Zionist movement, for whose fulfillment he struggled until his early death in 1904. His idea lived on among his followers.

In 1917 the English Secretary of State for Foreign Affairs, Lord Arthur Balfour, declared his country's intention of making Palestine the national home of the Jews. Chaim Weizman, the British, Russian-born chemist, had contributed to England's efforts in fighting World War I. His merit and influence played a role in the creation of the Balfour Declaration. After World War I, Britain asked the European states for the mandate over the little land of Palestine, an important central point between the Western world and Britain's Eastern and African colonies. The mandate, for the main purpose of establishing a Jewish homeland and the protection of the Palestinian Jews, was approved in 1920, ending the Turkish rule with the help of Jewish battalians under Vladimir Jabotinsky. Thus the Balfour Declaration of 1917 was implemented, twenty-five years after Herzl's first appeal for the establishment of a Jewish state.

However, at the start of the Second World War in 1939, when the need for a Jewish refuge was desperate, Britain issued the *White Paper*, catering to the wealthy Arab landowners and the powerful oil-rich Arab nations, encouraging the formation of an Arab League, and restricting further Jewish immigration under a quota system, which was to cease completely after 1944! The *White Paper*, which naturally aroused the bitterness and disappointment of Jews all over the world and, to be sure, did not reflect the attitude of the majority of the private British citizenry, totally disregarded the obligation of the mandate while the methodical massacre of Jews on the whole European continent was carried out by the Nazis.

How the British government lived up to her promise and obligation under the mandate is amply demonstrated by the loss of thousands of Jewish lives due to her shameful hostility toward the passengers of some rickety boats, trying to enter Palestine. In 1940 the *Patria*, which carried nearly two thousand Jewish refugees, was prevented from landing on Palestine's shore by British navy men. Hundreds of refugees ended up on the bottom of the ocean (two of them from my hometown were among the lucky ones who managed to swim ashore; some last souvenirs from my parents trapped in Germany before their deportation, a few personal photographs, were lost in that tragedy).

In 1942 a leaky old Rumanian boat, the *Struma*, whose passengers were hoping in vain for British certificates to enter Palestine, remained for two months off the Turkish coast, then was forced to return to Europe. On the way back to death, the vessel was torpedoed and exploded, and all eight hundred passengers except two were killed.

After India obtained independence and, shortly after, all British troops had to be withdrawn from Egypt, Britain was determined to maintain her hold on Palestine. English officers continued to prevent Jews from entering the country and stirred up the Arabs to fight the Jews. The combined forces of the *Haganah*—the legal defense army of the Palestine Jews—and the members of the kibbutzim sometimes succeeded in outwitting the British patrols and enabled a number of refugees to swim ashore and enter the country. Many hundreds of others were shipped to concentration camps on Mauritius and Cyprus by the British.

In the turbulent times from 1945 to 1948, the Jewish population was exposed to much suffering and many interruptions of their daily routine due to the cruel policy of the British, and a lot of heroism and patriotism was displayed by various groups. Several teenagers, members of a militant party, condemned to be hanged for their retaliation for British brutalities and executions, were known to have marched singing to the gallows.

Frequent curfews were imposed by the English. Once, interrupting a short summer vacation in Jerusalem, the "Switzerland" of Palestine, I traveled to my rented room in Tel Aviv to take care of a matter relating to my teaching position, intending to return to Jerusalem that evening. Before reaching home, I heard loudspeakers announcing a curfew of indefinite duration as a penalty for the whole Tel Aviv population. Anyone found outside or seen at a window would immediately be shot. I rushed to the safety of my room, where I had *nothing* in the way of food or drink! The couple from whom I had rented the room were either away or, as happened occasionally, we were not on speaking terms. Assuming that one day's fasting would not do me any harm, I hoped for the curfew to end soon. I thought of medical emergencies—cardiac patients, women in labor, and the like.

On the second day, the gnawing hunger and the uncertainty began to bother me. I vaguely remembered having met a woman in the rear building of the double house, and grabbing a cup, I waited till no plane or copter was overhead and hurriedly crossed the atrium between the front and rear buildings. With my treasure of a small piece of bread and a cupful of quaker oats, I safely reached my room again and managed to survive three days, after which the curfew ended.

A few weeks later, walking one afternoon around the corner toward the grocery, I narrowly escaped being hit by a shell or mine exploding very near me in the street!

The adventures told about the heroism, patriotism, and resourcefulness of the Jewish fighters of that period beat many a mystery story. Once when I was staying with friends in Ramat Aviv, they had a visitor, whose story they told me later. On a train, handcuffed, escorted by two English officers to his trial, he had one advantage over them: his thorough knowledge of the train and the territory. Before they were approaching a bend on the way, he asked to be escorted to the bathroom. Both stood outside, closely watching the scene through the window, lest he try to escape. Realizing that he had one chance to save his life by jumping out the window exactly at the bend where they could not watch him for a few seconds, he escaped and survived.

On November 27, 1947, the United Nations finally took a vote on the fate of Palestine. Partition was agreed upon, and Britain had to give up the mandate and leave Palestine within a few months. Jewish hopes ran high, despite the still restricted immigration and the tiny state assigned to the Jewish sector led by David Ben-Gurion, head of the Jewish Agency. But the Arabs, incited against the Jews by both the British and the Nazi-sympathizing leaders of the Arab League, opposed the partition and started the war. Another Holocaust threatened. The United States immediately voted for the partition plan, followed by Russia two days later. Then the U.S. government suddenly reversed its support. In this fight of David against Goliath during those fateful years of 1945–1948, the Jews in the United States offered considerable help to their brothers in Palestine and to those endangered in Arab countries, and they were active to reestablish the lives of death-camp survivors, many of whom were terminally ill.

In 1948, at the zenith of the war, all able-bodied persons were called up to enlist for army duty. Female teachers were sometimes exempt since they were responsible for the safety of their students. There was a desperate shortage of arms and ammunition in the Jewish sector. In the Sharon Valley, according to my friends, there was one gun to every seven men at the front! But the Jews knew what they were fighting for, whereas the Arabs fought mostly under orders of their rich landowners.

In Tel Aviv, most air attacks being at night, we spent hours during many nights in the cellar, which served as our air-raid shelter. I remember one night, when a bomb did not hit its objective vertically, but fell sideways into an air-raid shelter at the corner of Montefiore and Allenby Streets, two blocks from where I lived. All the people in the shelter were killed instantly. In one daytime air attack of Tel Aviv, one hundred persons were killed and many more wounded. A certain M. L., an old Zionist from my hometown, was listed among the casualties. A few weeks later, to my surprise and joy, I met him in the street, resurrected, unharmed, his usual cheerful self. He explained that his namesake M. L. was the victim, and that, according to legend, after all the rumors, he himself was to he blessed with a very long life.

In late 1947 and early 1948 the settlements and kibbutzim outside Jerusalem were attacked by Arabs, and all the residents who had not fled were murdered in the most bloodcurdling way. All the young settlers of the fairly new Orthodox Kfar Etzion suffered this tragic fate.

Then began the siege of Jerusalem, where all communications and supplies ceased. There seemed to be no way to save the trapped, starving, incessantly bombed Jewish population of this city.

After many vain arduous attempts to break through the massive military buildup of the barricades preventing any access to the Jewish city of Jerusalem, the combined forces of the *Haganah* and the militant sections of the army—the *Irgun* and the Stern Group—found a secret backroad, later called the "Burma Road," to reach the Holy City, which was thus miraculously saved at last!

One of those who lost their lives during the siege was the aged father of a science teacher, one of my colleagues. He had been standing inside the doorway of the Jerusalem apartment house where he lived, waiting for his tiny ration of milk and water, when a bullet killed him.

Two hundred thousand Arabs had fled from Jaffa and other Palestinian territories. But the Jews announced that all peaceable Arabs were welcome to return and resume their homes and property. Only a few thousand followed this call. They were urged by their leaders to run—where??! The many large surrounding Arab countries, some sparesely populated, closed their borders to their brothers. Instead, they used the poor, frustrated, embittered refugees in the crowded camps in or bordering on Israel to incite them as well as world opinion against the State of Israel, which they blamed for their plight, following the evil methods of slanderous Nazi refugees, who had become honored citizens in some Arab countries.

At the same time, during and shortly after the War of Independence, the Jewish residents in Yemen were in grave danger. With the help of American Jews, they were saved by being airlifted to the new State of Israel, where they were welcomed and absorbed.

On May 15, 1948, while the fighting continued, the sovereign Jewish state was proclaimed in Tel Aviv under the name of ISRAEL, which was the name given to the biblical Jacob by God's Angel. David Ben-Gurion was elected as premier, and Chaim Weizman as the first president. In May of 1949, the State of Israel, somewhat larger than under the Partition Plan, was admitted to the United Nations.

ELEVEN

SIX
NATIONAL
ANTHEMS!

The world, beyond a reasonable doubt, is one of the most interesting places. Being driven by the *Wanderlust* to roam the globe, "to strive, to seek, to find, and not to yield," as the poet Alfred, Lord Tennyson says in "Ulysses," enjoying gorgeous sceneries, various climates, cultures, and customs, is a fascinating pastime, one of the ten pleasures in life.

An altogether different situation arises when one is not a tourist or a visitor on temporary assignment, but a victim of persecution having fled from one's natural habitat, one's homeland on the Hitler-dominated European continent, to find a refuge, a livelihood, a new career, and new friends in an unknown country. A language barrier would sometimes present an additional hardship.

Those of us who grew up in Germany near the French border heard the *Marseillaise* sung occasionally during the years following World War I. As I learned later, there were certain "Separatists" who wanted the left Rhineland, which had changed hands several times in history, to become permanently French. Their voices were soon silenced as "treasonous" by the German majority.

Growing up in democratic Germany and then under the barbarian Hitler regime was like living in two different countries, even before the radical persecution of the Jews. The national anthems used by the old and the new governments reflect the contrast between the civilized spirit of "Deutschland über alles" and the martial, vulgar approach of the Nazi Party anthem which replaced it since 1933, the ill-famed Horst-Wessel Lied, which was named after its "poet" and composer, who was killed in a street brawl three years before Hitler came to power. The text of the *Deutschlandlied*, watered down from a poem by the medieval minnesinger Walther von der Vogelweide,[1] was worded by the nineteenth-century minstrel Hoffmann von Fallersleben, with the tune by Haydn. In 1922 it was decreed as the official German national anthem by President Hindenburg. As to Horst Wessel, it is not clear whether all the disgusting textual variants were his brainchildren, or whether he picked up some of the barbarisms at the dingy favorite haunt of the early Nazis, the Hamburg harbor pub. One refrain which I remember from my childhood was "Wenn's Judenblut vom Messer spritzt,/ Dann fühlen wir uns wohl." ("When Jewish blood drips from our knife,/ That's when we feel at ease.")

According to Dr. Franklin H. Littell, professor of religion at Temple University, most people and the churches in Germany knew about the fate of the Jews, but "kept quiet out of fear, while the professionals turned barbarians without conscience and murdered millions. . . . Most Christians ran like yellow dogs and left the Jews exposed. Most supported Nazism, and the Jews paid the price." He calls the Holocaust "the Christian religious crisis of the century."[2] Certainly, everybody had heard, just as I did, the Nazi text quoted above.

In 1949 the German Democratic Republic introduced its own solemn national anthem; the poet as well as the composer were veteran communists. After reunification of West and East Germany on October 3, 1990, the national anthem of West Germany was retained.[3]

Hard work has always been a German tradition. In our school, the guideline was Goethe's work ethic, his *Leistungsprinzip*, epitomized in the famous verse,

> Sechzig Minuten hat die Stunde,
> Über tausend hat der Tag.
> Söhnchen, werde dir die Kunde,
> Was man alles leisten mag!

> (Sixty minutes has the hour,
> Over a thousand has the day.
> Sonny, be aware of
> All one can achieve!)

This hectic striving for achievement is in stark contrast to the much more relaxed, leisurely atmosphere which awaits a person entering France, especially before the dark days of the Second World War.

The *Marseillaise*, composed in tune as well as text by the army officer and poet Rouget de Lisle in 1795 in praise of *la gloire de la patrie* (the glory of the homeland), was adopted as the French national anthem after having been roared enthusiastically at the storming of the Tuileries during the French Revolution.[4] The rhythm, the text, and the melodious quality of the French language—which prevails even when one hears two cabbies shouting curses at one another—have made it a popular song worldwide, along with the equally widespread English anthem.

During my vacations I often visited my sister in the beautiful historic city of Strasbourg. A mixture of French and German was spoken at the time in the city and the villages of the surrounding Vosges Mountains, especially by German-born students and transients waiting for emigration to North or South America.

French patriotism is almost unique in that a Frenchman would often refuse to respond to a tourist's question in English, although they do encourage tourism. The love of their country is ever present; it overshadows and outlasts poverty and misery and abounds notwithstanding their criticism of the government and local institutions. They rather live in poverty in France than in affluence elsewhere. Right or wrong, "Vive la France!"

A sad, true story, luckily with a happy ending, may serve to illustrate the French people's deep attachment to their country.

In the late 1960s, a young, pretty teacher of French in our school spent her summer vacation in France. She was so captivated by their lifestyle and their *savoir-vivre* and she fell so deeply in love with a young Frenchman that she decided to abandon her tenured position, her family and friends, to return to France forever (she thought). She discussed her plan with me, knowing about my familiarity with that country. However, she approached me in the spirit, "My mind is made up, don't confuse me with facts!" As expected, she disregarded my three warnings that (a) nonuniversity grads' secretarial jobs, like that of her beloved, were very poorly paid in France, without prospects of promotion; (b) she, with her foreign non-French degree, would not get licensed and find no worthwhile position; and (c) if things went wrong, the young man in question would agree under no circumstances to leave his country and follow her to the United States (which she apparently had in mind).

This was unfortunately exactly what happened. After two and a half years of an intense struggle, giving some private lessons, facing poverty and an uncertain future, she was back home with two babies, without a husband, who had promised nothing and was only very mildly interested in his children. After a couple of years, being still young, efficient, and resilient, she found another teaching position and, eventually, another husband with his own children and, hopefully, lived happily ever after.

After the mostly extroverted character of the French, one meets the restrained, courteous British with their typical understatement, which is also alien to the frequently self-aggrandizing, sometimes boisterous, and, under the fascist rule, even bombastic German style. Most British civilians are proudly aware that they don't have to shout to assert themselves or to wear their patriotism, albeit very proud, openly on their sleeves. Discomfort, pain, or an almost hopeless situation may be said to be "not too bad," "not quite up to par," and the like; brilliant, excellent achievement will be "pretty good" or just "all right." Emo-

tional outbursts are considered bad manners, an attitude
instilled early in children at boarding schools. Perhaps this
self-control and equanimity in the face of adversity,
regarding the personal as well as the political arena, has
contributed to Britain's success in maintaining her status as
a world power over many centuries.

The English national anthem, sung at any public event,
even at the movies, is a deferential tribute to their beloved
monarch, who had long ceased to wield any political
power even before World War II. Both the author and composer of the anthem are unknown. The words were first
printed in 1745 in *Gentleman's Magazine*, and the solemn
tune was adopted over many centuries by various countries
and used by several famous composers with similar texts,
each catering to the respective monarch.[5]

While becoming one of the family, with my daily routine of domestic duties prescribed, allowing me little outside contact, I could not help noticing what went on in the
micro- and macrocosm around me. I met many of the
second- and third-generation Jewish-British families,
descendants from East European immigrants. I came to
admire their close-knit, mutually supportive, alert mentality, so different, it seemed to me, from the more passive,
assimilated German Jews. Here they were acting in concert, quickly, fearlessly, in threatening situations, like
demonstrations scheduled by the Nazi sympathizer Sir
Oswald Mosley.

After years of waiting, I was informed in late 1939 that
my student certificate for Palestine was available. I crossed
the seas covered with mines and arrived in early 1940,
when the Arab hostilities against the Jews were still freshly

in everybody's mind. On the boat, an English lady, my Ping-Pong partner, had offered me a substitute math teacher's job for six weeks at an English school with Arabic students in Jaffa, a city fascinating to me, knowing about the recent clashes and the still lingering danger only from printed reports. I enjoyed my walks through the Arab quarters, so like the stories which I remembered from *Arabian Nights*. At the Department of Education in Tel Aviv, where I promptly applied for an English teaching position, my well-prepared "fluent" Hebrew one week after entering the country, and even more so, my "daring" in walking around in Jaffa alone, unarmed and unharmed, earned me a good deal of admiration. The fact is that what was interpreted as my "courage" only resulted from my inexperience and ignorance of the danger, as is sometimes the case.

My substitute position being finished with the arrival of the permanent math teacher, I enrolled in Hebrew literature, math, and whatever English was offered at the limited department, at the Hebrew University in Jerusalem, living with a friend and her father for some time, while teaching math and English private lessons and part-time school classes.

Before leaving England, I was interviewed by the first female British Reform Rabbi, Lady Montague, who confirmed what I had heard before, "If you immigrate in the United States, learn Hebrew for a teaching position; if in Palestine, English." She was right. After several months, I obtained a full-time English teaching position.

Upon entering Palestine, Jewish immigrants were immediately granted citizenship by the Jewish National Assembly. The meaning of the Hebrew national anthem, the "Hatikvah" ("The Hope"), had always been in the minds of religious Jews, as is evidenced in the conclusion of the Passover Seder* ("Next Year in Jerusalem!") long before Israeli statehood. The text of the "Hatikvah," which we had sung for years at meetings of the *Hechalutz* and the Zionist Organization, is ascribed to Naftali Herz Imber (1856–1909), and the tune to the cantor Nissan Belzer or the pioneer settler Samuel Cohen (dates of birth and death unknown). It was adopted as the national anthem in 1948.[6]

Palestine/Israel was and is, from any aspect, a fascinating place historically, politically, culturally, religiously, ethnically, demographically, scenically, and archeologically. The profound patriotism of most Jews in the new homeland was not only deeply rooted in religion and history, but also in the knowledge that this was the only place where they were welcome and could hope, despite increasing restrictions imposed by the British, to find a refuge from the Nazi massacres in Europe.

One superbly organized field in the country is education, which has to overcome the major challenge of the demographic multiculturalism. Schooling is understood, by the Jewish authorities and private citizens alike, to be of the utmost importance as a preparation for life—for learning a profession or trade, earning a livelihood, and social status. Any teacher who is productive and preparing the large classes—many of fifty to fifty-five students—successfully for the official examinations is respected, honored, promoted, and catered to.

One of the professional groups faced with adjustment

---

*A Jewish service held on the first two evenings of Passover in commemoration of the exodus from Egypt.

problems early were the many immigrant medical doctors from several European countries during the 1930s. Unlike foreign physicians entering the United States, doctors arriving in Palestine could immediately open a practice on the basis of their German, Austrian, Polish, Swiss, Italian, or other license without additional training and exams. In my hometown, during my childhood, we had one family doctor, who made no errors in his diagnoses and therapies, whom we trusted completely. It was unwise to apply this attitude to all newly arrived European physicians, to most of whom, like in the rest of the world, gastroenterology in general and (sub)-tropical bacteriology and parasitology were "virgin soil where no human hand had ever set foot." I remember vividly that for a digestive problem one doctor always prescribed a generous dose of castor oil, another applied the strangest procedures, still others declared in stentorian tones that the patient suffered from "nervous stomach." In time a patient was sometimes lucky to find a knowledgeable and caring doctor. All this, no doubt, has changed in the meantime.

In the summer of 1954 I accepted an invitation from my relatives in Philadelphia, took a year's sabbatical leave from my English high-school position in Tel Aviv (which was extended to two years), and enrolled in the English Department of Temple University for my Master's degree. At the same time, I taught Hebrew at a religious school. I always found the U.S. authorities and the professors very courteous, respectful, fair, and helpful. The two not altogether pleasant surprises were some previous misinformation by my relatives and the hot, humid summer climate of Philadelphia, where I missed the sea breeze of Tel Aviv.

In the public school position, which I held for many years, I taught English (my major by my choice) and German, Latin, French, and Hebrew alternately. During my tenure in that school district, I met several representatives at the highest echelon of the New York State Education Department, who were appreciative of my credentials and singled me out time and time again for referral of student teachers preparing for junior or senior high-school English. They first attended my classes for a few weeks and then fulfilled their practice teaching requirement under my supervision during the last semester of their bachelor's degree program. Some of them stayed in touch long after having obtained their first high-school job. This U.S. student-teaching requirement on the college level is an excellent program, not available in most European countries, as far as I know, where it deserves to be introduced.

On the other hand, the usefulness of the innumerable education courses at American universities, whether required or voluntary, is more than questionable. For permanent certification, I had to take several of them for my various subjects. The advantage was that, at our regular after-class coffee-table, I met some very bright African American students, professors at Southern universities for black enrollees, and I learned a lot about their "numerus nullus" (nonadmittance) to "white" universities, the ongoing discrimination, and the very low salaries of these professors. At the time of this writing, these practices have long been declared illegal and have disappeared.

What had apparently not disappeared many years after the war were certain deep-seated anti-Semitic and pro-Nazi trends which I witnessed several times. One aged German high-school teacher had the nerve to inform me that she had strongly objected when, before and early during World War II, the members of the American German Teachers Association had decided by majority vote to send a petition signed by many hundreds of members to the German Embassy protesting the anti-Semitic laws and the violence against the Jews. She declared that she had always been opposed to teachers organizations' involvement in politics, which she considered unprofessional and, in this case, likely to harm U.S.-German relations.

Some years later I heard a German-born professor complain about the lack of compassion that people showed her, although she felt that she deserved as much sympathy as any Jewish Holocaust survivor. After all, she did not start World War II, in which her brother was wounded, and she often went hungry and spent many nights in air-raid shelters!

How indelibly Nazi doctrines are ingrained in former party members' mentality, I found evidenced by several incidents during and after my publications and doctoral studies. For instance, when we spoke once about literary anthologies, I made an observation to the chairman of a German Department about a German-born publisher and his, as I phrased it, "typically German arrogance." The professor's answer was, "But he isn't German at all! He is a Jew!" ("Aber er ist ja gar kein Deutscher! Er ist ja Jude!") Other anti-Jewish, biased actions of his followed.

Needless to mention, I had memorized the text of the Pledge of Allegiance and "The Star-Spangled Banner," the origin of which goes back to eighteenth-century England, and the words and music of which were officially designated as the United States National Anthem by Congress and President Hoover in 1931.[7] For the first time since leaving Germany, I noticed that discrimination and bias against religious affiliation and country of origin were not dead. I heard of cases of anti-Semitism in my neighborhood and of vandalism against some synagogues in the county. At my school I found my new principal sometimes staring at me during the Pledge of Allegiance and the anthem.

In some states the requirements for principals and other high-level administrators are still largely confined to "education" courses so that, instead of being experts in one or two subjects, they have attended a plethora of repetitious technical courses. Those who are ambitious can write a dissertation on administrative questions, such as scheduling, syllabi, or attendance-taking, for a doctorate of education (Ed.D.). These college and "in-service" courses are usually well filled, for they lead to better positions in the burgeoning hierarchy and to salary increments. In these programs the "inverted pyramid" is emphasized, where the teacher is pictured all the way at the bottom, and those who have succeeded in getting out of the classroom pressure into the easier, better paid, more respected administrative positions are in charge of supervising, coordinating, hiring and firing. On the other hand, many parents are well aware of productive teachers' importance, to whose classes they often want their children assigned. In teacher preparation, studies in subject matter should also be more emphasized. One cannot teach what one does not know! Gradually, under taxpayers' pressure, administrations and teacher training are being adjusted to the changing needs in education, and certification requirements are becoming stricter. Conversely, it is questionable whether remediation courses in the three Rs belong on the college level!

As soon as I had my driver's license, I roamed this incredibly beautiful country far and wide. After the, at that time, still rather barren stretches of Israel, with a particular beauty of their own, I was struck by the lush green, the formidable mountains, the chasms, canyons, geysers, caves, and caverns, the boundless streams and lakes, compared with that tiny country sharing the one Jordan River with a neighboring state, and a couple or wadis, where every drop of water is precious. Later, I was especially fascinated by the innumerable bridges in various shapes, each adapted to the gorgeous scenery as if it had grown naturally, and yet, each an architectural work of art. I never tired of immortalizing them with my camera. Why do American tourists never talk of the unique scenic beauty of this country, which has everything, I wondered. Don't they know how blessed they are? When, many years later, I was interviewed in Amsterdam, I was told, "You are quite an exception: Americans hardly ever mention the beauty of their country."

Another puzzling question comes to mind: Wherever there is poverty, famine, strife, global or civil war, oppression, and aggression, the world looks to America for compassion, help, financial support, all of which are often readily provided, in kind and human resources, to countries in need. Are the help, charity, and generosity of this country in sharing her wealth ever genuinely appreciated by the recipient governments? Why is it that this hand that feeds others is sometimes bitten, and what causes such arrogance and lack of gratitude? Is it envy or, what one author termed "The Anxiety of Influence"?[8]

You may ask: How can a person be expected to be a loyal, reliable, and well-adjusted citizen in each of several different countries, law abiding and productive under various forms of government? The answer is fairly simple: One must learn to master the language, read a daily newspaper, make adjustments if one does not want to remain a stranger and live in a self-imposed cultural ghetto.

Many celebrities, such as Albert Einstein, Thomas Mann, Martin Buber, Marlene Dietrich, and Max Brod, lived in four, five, or six countries after their native land was taken over by Hitler, and they became *citoyens du monde* (citizens of the world). If someone is responsible, loyal, and productive by nature and upbringing, that individual will adhere to these characteristics wherever (s)he lives. One can find kind, helpful, well-meaning individuals everywhere, as well as conniving, jealous, insiduous, advantage-taking persons. If parents and educators do their duty preparing those in their charge for life, young people will be fit for decision making, fulfilling their task, and shaping their fate.

Like the protagonist of Oliver Goldsmith's novel *The Vicar of Wakefield*, the writer of this text was ill-prepared for the world and realized late in life having made the mistake of being much too trusting toward the wrong people. One pays the price and, more often than not, survives.

TWELVE

VISITING JEWISH MEMORIALS IN "NEW" EUROPE

I n the fall of 1990, I decided to join a guided tour of several Eastern European countries after the Communist collapse. One of my major objectives was to see the remnants of Jewish culture in the Eastern bloc countries. With that goal in mind, I booked for a coach tour leading through eleven cities in seven countries.

After a long night flight, we arrived in Budapest, very hot despite the early morning hour. While waiting at the airport for the formalities connected with some participants' missing luggage, I strolled around and soon noticed a group of eighty-nine newly arrived Russian émigrés—among them thirty children—guarded by Hungarian military police. They were just boarding a bus transporting them to a nearby El-Al plane. There was no chance to talk to them. I later learned that there are presently 89,000 Jews residing in Hungary.

Parts of this chapter were originally printed in *Martyrdom and Resistance* (September/October 1991): 15–16. It is used with the publisher's permission.

After a long, bumpy ride we arrived in historic Krakau, which had largely been spared the ravages of Hitler's war. The city was teeming with tourists, especially Japanese, who were thronging the booths of the fleamarket arcades selling the local specialties of amber jewelry and laces.

Our group consisted of forty-one passengers, eight of them Jewish (one of them, a lady married to a Jew, had converted to Judaism), plus our Yugoslav escort and various guides, all of whom spoke a more or less phonetic English. To my (and our Catholic escort's) surprise, almost all the passengers requested the time-consuming optional trip to the Oświencim death camp.

At the entrance, the over-life-size chained skeletal metal figure embodies the inhuman suffering and abysmal despair of the prisoners. After a brief film, we walked through the countless horror chambers, incredulously viewing the methodically separated mountains of faded clothes, shoes, hair, dentures, little suitcases, protheses, eyeglasses—anything that apparently promised some gain to the destroyers. For instance, "Hair was sold at 50 Pfennig one kilogramme."[1] The sights and displays, combined with the matter-of-fact detailed account of the local guide, outdid any previous reports, descriptions, and pictures of the mass sadism by the SS and the unheard-of suffering of the inmates. Walking along the endless cobblestone streets, I remembered the words of Pastor Niemöller, one of the German clergymen who had the guts, in his church sermons, to warn a nation, intoxicated by Hitler's promises, against Nazi doctrines, before he himself was thrown into the Dachau Camp:

First they came for the Jews. I was silent. I was not a
Jew.
>Then they came for the Communists. I was silent. I
was not a Communist.
>Then they came for the trade-unionists. I was silent.
I was not a trade-unionist.
>Then they came for me. There was no one left to
speak for me.

Reverend Niemöller was no doubt aware that the Jewish-
born Jesus, had he been alive, would have been a victim of
Nazi persecution. A certain number of prisoners were usually chosen to form a special detachment ("Sonderkom-
mando") to empty the gas chambers and to burn the
corpses. Being in the know, they, too, would be sent to gas
chambers after some time and they would be replaced by
prisoners from a fresh transport.[2]

In spite of the fact that things were kept in the utmost
secrecy, one member of the special squad managed to
make notes of several events. The notes were hidden in a
glass jar and buried underground. Among them the mass
murders of children are mentioned:

The children were so pretty, . . . so well-made, that it
was striking, when compared with the rags they were
covered with. . . . In the second half of October 1944,
. . . the children realized that they were being led to their
death. They began running hither and thither in the yard,
in a dead fright, clutching their heads in despair.[3]

The horror at the enormity of this catastrophe is too
deep for tears, especially after the lapse of half a century.

Once, however, after my trip, I could not hold back the tears, remembering the mountains of tiny baby shoes and clothes displayed at the gruesome Auschwitz Museum; it was when I happened to watch a TV show which dealt with the plight of the neglected Rumanian orphans and the hundreds of American families lining up eagerly to welcome the Rumanian children whom they had volunteered to adopt. While my heart went out to those orphans, I could not help thinking of the million or more Jewish children starved and murdered by the Nazis. Where were the American and European volunteers then, and where was the international Red Cross, so easily fooled during their ONE visit at Theresienstadt, the "concentration camp resort," for inspection of the Nazis' phony show, while the whole world knew already what went on?!

Reading the documented U.S. immigration policies and laws at the entrance of the Ellis Island Museum, which I toured a few years ago, I found the following text printed in huge letters:

THE US GOVERNMENT PURSUES AN INFLEX-
IBLE POLICY OF DENYING REFUGE TO THE
MANY EUROPEANS FLEEING NAZI PERSECU-
TION. IN 1939, FOR EXAMPLE, CONGRESS RE-
FUSES TO CONSIDER AN EXCEPTION TO THE
IMMIGRATION LAW THAT WOULD ADMIT 20,000
GERMAN CHILDREN, MOST OF THEM JEWISH.

The countless Auschwitz visitors from all over the globe were pale and silent, as was our group back on the bus, except for a handful of older women who had perhaps felt unable to do all the walking. They had apparently used the time to purchase some jewelry in the village of Oświencim; their voices sounded grotesquely unreal when they showed each other their bargains in the back of the bus.

On to beautiful, rebuilt Warsaw. Our rigid schedule permitted hardly any contact with the population, except for hotel employees, here and there a waiter or salesperson, and our tour guides. The answer to my question about the Polish people's attitude to the pending reunification of Germany was invariably that they were scared, based on their or their family's experience at the outbreak of World War II.

Included in our itinerary was a visit to a small restored synagogue with four little old Jewish people, apparently Holocaust survivors. The guide told us that of the millions of former Polish Jews, who had made up half the population of Warsaw, there were now two hundred elderly left in the nursing home.

Whether genuine or just patronizing, our Catholic Polish guides, noticing the questions and concern of some participants, exhibited a general interest in items of our Jewish heritage.

One of our next stops was the site of the former Warsaw Ghetto, which had been razed to the ground after the inmates' uprising, and which is now covered with several monuments bearing Hebrew inscriptions. Our special Polish (Catholic) guide, overhearing me reading and translating the texts to some bystanders, drew near and addressed me in fluent Hebrew. He told me that, to communicate with Israeli tourists, politicians, and the like, he had taken twenty computer lessons in everyday Hebrew, and to reinforce them, he had vacationed in Israel. He seemed thrilled to have the opportunity to add a few words to his vocabulary, and he availed himself of every chance to exchange some sentences.

East Berlin, with its abundant historic treasures, museums, and restored architecture, was far more interesting than modern, rebuilt West Berlin. The leftover part of the Wall with its bizarre graffiti was one of the major attractions. No one seemed to know how many Jews had settled in the city, since they were scattered in various parts.

After Meissen and Dresden, having crossed the border into Czechoslovakia, we made a short stop at the Terezin (Theresienstadt) camp site. Some of us walked the ten-minute distance along the road to the camp, on which no vehicles were allowed. As far as the eye could see, the ground was covered right and left with vast horizontal expanses densely engraved with the names and places of origin of millions upon millions of deceased. The place was crowded with tourists. In vain did I try to detect the name of my grandmother, who had perished there. At age 80, shortly after a hip fracture, she was deported to Theresienstadt, where she died after three weeks of starvation and sickness, as her grandson's research revealed.[4] We were given no time to step inside, beyond the sign "ARBEIT MACHT FREI."[5]

In Prague we visited Europe's oldest synagogue, site of many legends, and the crowded, overgrown cemetery, both devoid of worshipers, since, like in most other European countries, there are hardly any Jewish residents here after the twelve years of Hitler's "Thousand-Year Reich of World Dominance." In keeping with an old Jewish tradition, rocks had been placed on the monuments instead of flowers.

140

The neglected, overgrown graves conjured up in my mind the small Jewish cemetery in Trier, my native city, which I had visited many years ago. I had cleared away the weeds from my father's grave, to which we had added a stone for my mother. Nearby was the tomb of the war-blind Mr. S., bearing the accusing inscription of his murder in Auschwitz after having given his eyesight for the fatherland. Added to my traumatic experience of my cemetery visit were the signs on the stores, long ago "Aryanized," in the still lively business section. Under the names of the present owners were those familiar to me from my childhood, painted in large letters, for example, "FORMERLY X.Y.," or "FOUNDED 1880 by J. C. & SONS," or the like—apparently in an attempt to atone for the enormity of the crime committed against the Jewish residents.

One comforting event was meeting a former friend and classmate, to whom I was referred by a storeowner. We have kept up contact since. She told me that one of my favorite high-school teachers for many years, who taught us French and Middle-High German, having survived both world wars unscathed, committed suicide in 1945 because he could not bear the shame of the renewed defeat and the division of his beloved country. I also heard that my brilliant piano teacher, a disciple of the famous Italian composer Ferruccio Benvenuto Busoni, had been murdered in a death camp. She had left Prague in the 1920s with her children and her husband, who became a tenor in our city opera, but passed away. Hearing about the planned deportation of persons "without nationality" by the Nazis, she fled with her two daughters to Paris, where she and her elder daughter were arrested and shipped to their extermination. Like for so many millions, there was no gravestone, no mourners. The younger daughter did survive in Vichy France, but lost her two husbands, one after the other, each returning deathly sick from a German slave-labor camp.

In Vienna our guide was a young woman who had never heard about her head of government, Kurt Waldheim, being denied entry into the United States, let alone the reason for this measure. I had visited the "Judendorf" near the Baden spa in the early 1980s and I did not do much sightseeing this time, especially since I would have preferred to bypass Austria. Our last stop was Zagreb, with lots of military police all over the city, to keep the peace among the turbulent four ethnic factions. It was the beginning of many years of civil war and brutal "ethnic cleansing," which even our Yugoslav escort apparently did not foresee.

At the end of the tour, I was left with the vague hope and with a dream that the bloodstained lesson of history and the cataclysmic experience of our own generation might someday result in counteracting any continuing prejudice and racism in our midst and a gradual implementation of a peaceful coexistence in tiny, war-torn Israel.

THIRTEEN

INTERLUDE IN LAS PALMAS

"**Y**ou will hear a lot of German spoken in Gran Canaría, also some English and French, and of course, Spanish," the travel agent informed me. I pondered about the remark for a moment, but brushed it aside. I seldom had an opportunity to use German, which was, after all, not only the medium of the Hitler gangsters; it was also the language of some of the most brilliant and noble minds in human history—Lessing, Goethe, Schiller, Kant, Heine, Kafka, Musil, and so many others. I am said to be a workaholic, engrossed in my professional career, some charitable activities, and writing. Feeling claustrophobia closing in on me after a heavy schedule and being unable to obtain Caribbean accommodations at short notice, I quickly decided in mid-December, a few years ago, to recharge my batteries for the spring by escaping for a week to the sunny Canary Islands.

The day after my arrival in Las Palmas, no swimming

weather. I did not expect an eventful New Year's evening after dinner in the plush hotel. So I walked for many hours and did some shopping at El Corte Inglés, La Gallería, and the kiosks between them. On my way back I noticed the section of the island which is inhabited by Germans, used for their winter residence. Back in the hotel, I heard mostly Spanish spoken and some German. I must have been on my feet for eight hours, and jet lag began to overcome me while I got ready for the late dinner.

Joining the waiting line outside the festive, decorated dining hall, I noticed the guests in their formal evening attire and regretted having adhered to my habit, before traveling overseas, of packing the plainest, most casual outfits that I could find. It was too late now to feel self-conscious about my simple green-and-white sports outfit, dressed up a bit with accessories. I soon found myself chatting with a young Scottish couple, just arrived that afternoon. The doors opened, and I was escorted to a table for one. The feast proceeded, with delectable dishes, unlimited refills of red and white wine, champagne, noisemakers, and the rest, Spanish and international, to herald the new year. One couple, apparently trying to chisel their way in, was quickly whisked away from a table nearby; the vacancy was filled pronto with another couple, Swedish or Dutch, it seemed, to whom a tall, distinguished-looking gentleman, grey-haired with a young face, was added, there being no more tables for one available. The atmosphere grew progressively noisier and more relaxed, and the food, drink, glittering gifts, and photographers made the guests feel like old friends, laughing, waving, chatting, and twittering among the tables. The only seemingly deaf-mute diners were the three guests at the table near mine. At one point the distinguished-looking gentleman at that table said something to me in French about the quality of the red and white wines, to which I replied in the same language. That is how it started.

His face lit up, he seemed so happy to have found someone to talk to in a common language. After dessert the couple at his table withdrew, and he asked to join me at my table. He proved to be charming company, amusing, polished, and sophisticated, at the same time warm and frank with his boyish smile, so eager to have fun and to communicate. We opened the colorful bags and tried on the hats, noses, and other accoutrements—everything fitted to perfection. Again I regretted not being dressed more appropriately for the occasion. Soon we were on the crowded dance floor—he was very good at that, too, even the Latin numbers, and he complimented me on the ease with which he could talk to me. Forgotten were my jet lag and fatigue.

I learned that he was German, had two grown children and a wife (he did not seem to care in whose company she spent New Year's Eve). What a bizarre situation, I thought, finding myself dancing with a German of all people and enjoying his company. We sat down again. He spoke about his past and future, his co-ownership of a company, with branches in several parts of Germany, adjoining countries, and America, and his plans to expand their export further. He gave me his card, asked for mine. He showed me his vacation reading in German translation, which he carried around, a book on finances by one Baron de Rothschild. Judging by his conversation, he was born around the early thirties. He discovered that I spoke German well—his had a southern lilt, as did his French.

We followed the crowd to the cocktail lounge. I listened to him, saw no opportunity at the moment to tell him about my varied European, British, Israeli background before settling down in the suburban New York area, about my professional activities. In the rush to watch the enormous champagne bottle at midnight, such personal details could wait, I felt, floating on the waves of champagne, music, brotherhood. On our way, arm-in-arm, to find a space among the crowds, he suggested to view the event from his or my room, drawing me closer to him. This was a bit unexpected to me, but nothing to get upset about. What upset me was the tremendous attraction which I felt for the combined looks and personality of this man, who had to be a member of that "master race"! He was quick to notice that I stiffened.

Being alone and very busy, living in a provincial area, I was sometimes asked about marriage, and I used to joke, "Nobody deserves me right now." How tempting to feel young again this New Year's Eve, to forget inhibitions, past and future, my rigidly disciplined pattern of life, and to abandon myself to the unexpected fun of the evening and his charming company. After all, he had been a child when it all happened in Europe.

Suddenly my alter ego raised its warning head and conjured up in my mind his Aryan Bavarian father and uncles in SS uniforms, crushing the world under their black boots in the goose-step march. What was I doing, flirting with a German, flattered by his attention and compliments? Shadows of the past appeared before my mind's eye, the silent procession of those close to me, victims of the most shameful chapter in German history, in fact, in world history,

146

whose images had haunted me for so many years in my dreams and waking hours—my parents and relatives, the friends of my youth, of Polish parentage, deported in late 1938 to starve and freeze to death in a no-man's-land between Germany and Poland. I turned to my partner and said, "I am Jewish, you know." He understood that much English and looked thoughtful for a moment after that piece of information, obviously unwarranted as far as he was concerned.

Then we were engulfed in the ocean of onlookers watching the famous champagne bottle pop open at the stroke of twelve amid the fireworks, with the "felicidad" hugs and kisses from all sides. I felt I had to get away for a few minutes from the sweetness of his presence. I excused myself, saying, "Cependant vous pourriez danser avec une de ces jeunes filles seules." ("Meanwhile you might dance with one of these young women who are alone.") He begged me to return. I promised.

On my way back, composed and sobered, I was intercepted and whirled around by an American, whose wife stood nearby, nodding and smiling at me. "She does not mind, for she does not dance," he explained. I saw the German dancing with a slender black lady, "charmante, du Sénégal" ("Charming, of Senegal"), he told me, when, the dance finished, he rejoined me. (A racist he apparently is not, I concluded.) He introduced me to his newly discovered German friends while I was away, a young couple, he a physician. The young man told us that he had studied classical languages and, unlike many other Germans, did not master French. So we chatted in German. After a brief conversation, the young doctor said, "Sie sprechen ja ein ausgezeichnetes Deutsch." ("You speak an excellent

German.") The music was very loud now. I noticed the doctor turn away from me to my escort, saying in a low voice, "Ich an Ihrer Stelle würde . . ." ("If I were you, I would . . ."). The rest was drowned in the bursts of music and laughter. After this, our conversation was formal and somewhat strained. Bewildered, as my partner seemed to be now, I soon excused myself and withdrew.

During the rest of the week, I made friends with two interesting British couples. Together, we took a fascinating whole-day tour to the surrounding mountains and craters and swam, weather permitting. What a story some of the guests had to tell when one got to know them closely! The one couple, obviously very much in love—an elegant, pretty petite woman and her husband, an engineer on a Saudi Arabian ship—were spending one of their occasional two-week honeymoons in Las Palmas, then had to separate again, she returning to her small town south of London, he to his ship. She, a Catholic, born and raised in South Africa, got married, had five children, divorced her husband, an alcoholic, and moved to England with her five children. To supplement her modest means, she worked as a waitress in a restaurant, where she met her husband, ten years younger than she. He had just obtained his engineering degree, and having no family ties anywhere at the time, being all alone, had accepted a well-paying position in the Saudi Arabian service. Born to Jewish parents in Warsaw when the Germans invaded Poland, his parents had given the baby, along with their savings, to a young Catholic couple before they themselves were locked up in the ghetto and perished. He had never even seen a picture of his parents. Apparently he had ended up in England with a children's transport after the war. He fell in love with the South African lady, they got married, and he adopted all her five children. Both their private lives were revolving around their letters and the two to three weeks a few times every year, which they could spend together.

On the beach I chatted a few hours with a young German history professor who had rented a lounge near mine. No problem there—no personal involvement. He easily opened up to me and told me about his vacation tours which he had guided to Spain, Russia, Israel. We talked in a potpourri of French, German, English, Latin, in which he proudly mingled a few words of Hebrew picked up in Tel Aviv. Chatting with him in several languages, I chuckled when I remembered how, a few years earlier, on an Alpine tour through several countries, one American traveler in my group, who lived in the Deep South, had asked me, only half-joking, "How come you speak all these languages like a native? Are you a spy?"

While listening to the young professor's strenuous efforts to communicate in Hebrew, I did some soul-searching of myself. I tried to take stock of the situation by analyzing my different responses to the two Germans. Why was I so ill at ease with my charismatic New Year's Eve partner and avoiding him, whereas I had no qualms socializing with the history professor? In the first case, I was practically swept off my feet by the perfect combination of looks, manners, intelligence, and sensitivity of the individual, which evoked unexpected romantic feelings in me, resulting in the ambivalent attraction and rejection. After half a century, was blaming a collective guilt on an individual member of a nation tantamount to prejudice on my part? Trying to solve the dilemma, I reasoned: With so many of my family, relatives, and friends wiped out when I was young, how could even the New Year's ambience of music, champagne, and dancing with the appealing companion, however personally innocent of the murdered millions, blot out, albeit temporarily, the terrible crime? Besides, my cultural heritage was still deeply ingrained in my bloodstream. My Orthodox upbringing had sometimes imposed restrictions upon me against which I rebelled, but there was also the fun of certain family gatherings, like the Seder and the Friday nights, with lots of unforgettable songs. I remembered the Zionist activities in my teens and the lives which I saved via foreign *hachsharah*, while I myself narrowly escaped being trapped in Germany to become another number in Hitler's "Final Solution" before finding refuge in an English domestic job shortly before World War II.

There was also the disturbing shadow of the sinister young doctor. Was it really all over? Or was it possible that the seeds which Hitler had sown long ago were sprouting and spreading again in the young generation?

I saw my New Year's Eve acquaintance a few times in the dining room. We were watching yet uneasily avoiding each other. We exchanged brief greetings and a few polite words. What went on in his mind, and in the stern young doctor's, I wondered. On my last evening, over an after-dinner farewell drink in the cocktail lounge with the English and the now so changed-looking Scottish couple (he proud of his deep, dark tan, his wife so light-colored, blonde, and freckled), I noticed the German watching us from the entrance, but he did not enter.

How could one ever forget?

FOURTEEN
AFTERWORD

NEVER AGAIN!!! was the worldwide outcry of the remaining Jews after Hitler's massacres, and of the non-Jews who had survived Hitler's wars. What have we learned since the end of World War II? True, neither before nor since the Second World War has there been a genocide of such dimensions. But there have been many more wars, more atrocities, more "ethnic cleansing" all over the world—in Africa, Asia, Central America, the Middle East, major terrorist attacks against the United States and Israel, and civil wars in Yugoslavia, which at this writing continues to be in the grip of racial and political hostilities.

The enormous technological developments, which could improve everyone's life on this planet, seem to be doomed in the hands of man to be turned into the grisly technology of killing. In the animal world, there is no choice: Predators and other species must kill for food so they and their genus can survive. Men, on the other hand, use their superior cerebral faculties to destroy each other frequently in human-made crises all over the globe. How can power-hungry dictators, who serve their own interests and disregard the public mandate, be stopped? The mad Neros who play the fiddle while Rome's slums are burning emerge time and time again.

What can we extrapolate from the present for the future of humankind? And what title will history assign to the twentieth century? Previous cultural epochs were characterized by generally accepted names such as Realism, Romanticism, the Renaissance, the Enlightenment or "The Age of Reason," the latter of which saw the gradual dawn of emancipation and the endowment of citizenship rights on the Jews, who had been exposed to attacks, pogroms, expulsion, and persecution throughout the ages. "They are used to it," claimed the Nazi leaders.

One widely known classic which captures the spirit of the Age of Reason is the timeless drama *Nathan der Weise* by the German playwright and philosopher Gotthold Ephraim Lessing (1729–1781). It contains a parable which is as valid today as it was at the time of its inception. The scene is Jerusalem, with Nathan, the Jew, the Sultan, a Moslem, and a young Knight Templar as the focal characters. Through their arguments and subsequent action the author expressed his plea for religious tolerance. The crucial concept is presented through a parable, which Nathan tells the Sultan, who has ordered the Jew to decide which of the three religions—Mohammedanism, Christianity, Judaism—is the true one. Nathan wisely tells the story of three rings, indistinguishable from one another, but one of them believed to have the grace of God and men to the wearer who believed in its virtue. The true ring was the one whose wearer proved its virtue by his own moral conduct throughout his life.

Other famous persons and rulers followed Lessing's example in their interest in the wisdom and high moral standards of the Jewish ghetto dwellers, among them Goethe, Frederick the Great in his regard for his frequent guest, the philosopher Moses Mendelsohn, and Queen Victoria's appointment of her prime minister and personal consultant Benjamin Disraeli.

Today, more than two hundred years later, what remains of the spirit of the Enlightenmnent? The author of the documentary *The Secret War against the Jews* suggests, as a title for the twentieth century, "The Age of Stupidity."[1] What prompted the author to decide on this title?

During the Cold War, which followed World War II, many of the most infamous war criminals were welcomed with open arms by several nations as anti-Communists, engineers, scientists, and others. They made a living and died peacefully of natural causes in their homes, in their beds, as citizens of their country of immigration. Some were recognized by a number of survivors, in whose very neighborhood they sometimes settled down, like in a certain case in the United States.[2] One of them, in charge of the mobile ground troops on the Russian front, devised a method by which he saved bullets in the massacres of many thousands of Jews. He ordered small children to be buried alive in prepared ditches, and he had adults wounded and then suffocated by dirt and bodies of the murdered being thrown on them. He was very proud of what he termed his "sardine method" and was subsequently promoted. To escape the noise of the slaughter, he left after the order and went for a ride. "He was a civilized man, after all. He even held a doctorate in the humanities from a Belgian university."[3]

After World War II one man traveled from Palestine to his native city in Latvia in search of his parents and siblings. He was told by some neighbors that one morning an SS officer ordered all Jewish men to assemble in the synagogue. He then locked the doors, had his soldiers pour gasoline around the foundation and set the building on fire. The women and children were cordoned off by the soldiers and had to watch the gruesome spectacle. They were later deported and massacred in various death camps.

During the War of Independence and the subsequent recognition needed from the world powers for Israeli statehood, some important surviving witnesses decided to concentrate on this vital goal for the time being rather than collect evidence to uncover the crimes against humanity by those grisly mass murderers and bring them to justice.

The second Holocaust was attempted after World War II against Israel and still is, by certain internal and external enemies, who are trying to convince the world powers that the murdered, not the murderers, are to blame: Israel has often been blamed for defense measures against terrorist attacks, which were aimed at undermining any peace process.

Finally, one memorable meeting deserves to be mentioned: It took place in June 1995 in a large hotel in the Catskill Mountains. Two hundred fifteen members of the Windmiller family, including 35 children and grandchildren and 12 guests (myself among them), arrived from 18 states in the United States and 11 distant countries. They gathered to pay tribute to the 172 family victims of the Holocaust, but also, at the same time, to celebrate life. The participants ranged from baby-age to an eighty-eight-year-old lady in a wheelchair. Among them were some death-camp survivors, each of whom reported about his or her incredible experiences.

One of the destructive results of the insane Nazi rule exemplified by this reunion was that families were torn apart and scattered all over the globe. But more important, the meeting also epitomized the spirit of vitality and resilience of the Jews and the failure of Hitler's "Final Solution."

Notwithstanding all the evidence of history's greatest crime, terrorist and revisionist hatemongers the world over cannot be silenced. One lecturer at the Islamic University in Gaza claimed in a Palestinian television broadcast on November 29, 2000, "No Dachau, no Chelmo, no Auschwitz! These were German disinfection centers. No Jew was murdered there!" A certain Gaza preacher, defending the lynching of two innocent Israelis by beating, stabbing, burning, and disemboweling them, then dragging their bodies through the streets, called on Palestinian television upon all Muslims "to butcher all Jews in any country, and those who stand by them."[4] This is hardly surprising when Palestinian leaders have constantly been using children as human shields in any fighting provoked by Arabs, so they can influence world opinion against Israel, "that shitty little country."[5]

As to the Palestinian claim to Jerusalem, which they insist is their religious "right": Jerusalem has been the Jewish capital since the time of King David. When religious Muslims get down on their hands and knees to pray five times a day, they turn their back on Jerusalem and face Mecca. "Jerusalem is mentioned in the Bible 700 times and not even once in the Koran," Asian scholar Dr. Ganchrow reminds us.[6]

Not only in primitive populations are hatemongers spreading their venom. For whatever self-serving reasons, Holocaust-denying revisionists have been busy in Western cultures, too. In the famous trial begun in London in the winter of 1999/2000 by revisionist David Irving against historian Prof. Deborah Lipstadt, the plaintiff, referring to the Auschwitz gas chambers as "a myth that will not die easily," sued Lipstadt for libel. The plaintiff was debunked by the most important witnesses, namely the Nazi perpetrators themselves in their meticulous diaries, speeches, and memoirs.

A partial entry of the powerful SS chief Heinrich Himmler's address to the SS generals in Posen, a province in Poland, on October 14, 1943, reads:

> I want to talk to you . . . on a very grave matter. Among ourselves it should be mentioned quite frankly, and we will never speak of it publicly. I mean . . . the extermination of the Jewish race. . . . Most of you know what it means when one hundred corpses are lying side by side, or five hundred, or one thousand. To have it out and at the same time . . . to have remained decent fellows, that is what has made us hard. This is a page of glory in our history which has never been written and is never to be written.[7]

One SS doctor wrote in his wartime diary during his first visit at Auschwitz, "August 29, 1942: By comparison, Dante's *Inferno* seems almost comedy!"[8]

NOTES

INTRODUCTION

1. Ian Kershaw, *Hitler: 1889–1936 Hubris* (New York: W. W. Norton, 1999), pp. 4–7.

2. Ibid., p. 18.

3. Adolf Hitler, *Mein Kampf*, 2 vols. in one, unabridged (Munich: Verlag Franz Eher Nachfolger, 1932), p. 271.

4. Ibid., p. 266.

5. Kazimierz Smolen et al., *Auschwitz 1940–45: Guidebook through the Museum*, trans. Krystina Michalik (Katowice: Krajowa Agencja Wydawnicza, 1981), p. 8. All attempts to obtain permission for use of a quotation or statement from this text were in vain: One letter was returned unopened, "Inconnu," another remained without response. Calls to the Polish Consulate in New York City were not answered.

CHAPTER 2

1. Himmler and other Nazi leaders boasted that they could identify a Jewish person from a distance of 50 meters.

2. See note 1 above.

3. On November 23, 1937, Hitler told the alumni of the SS Political School at Sonthofen, "The German people has the right to control the whole of Europe and to transform it into the Teutonic Reich of the German people." Archives of the weekly "Swiat" (World). Quoted in Kazimierz Smolen et al., *Auschwitz 1940–45: Guidebook through the Museum*, trans. Krystina Michalik (Katowice: Krajowa Agencja Wydawnicza, 1981), pp. 12–13.

CHAPTER 3

1. I was able to obtain additional information about my mother's fate from someone who interviewed a Kapo, a survivor, who had been put in charge of the Trier deportees in Lodz.

2. Rudolf Höss, *Death Dealer: The Memoirs of the SS Komandant at Auschwitz*, ed. Steven Paskuly, trans. Andrew Pollinger (Amherst, N.Y.: Prometheus Books, 1992), p. 363.

3. It is amazing that even in the death mill of Auschwitz, some secret illegal contact with the Polish resistance movement was maintained at extreme risk, for example, smuggling out and obtaining tiny hidden notes (Kazimierz Smolen et al., *Auschwitz 1940–45: Guidebook through the Museum*, trans. Krystina Michalik [Katowice: Krajowa Agencja Wydawnicza, 1981], pp. 88–92).

4. Höss, *Death Dealer*, p. 118.

5. Smolen et al., *Auschwitz 1940–45*, p. 12.

CHAPTER 5

1. Wiesenthal Center World Report, "History," *Response* (summer/fall 1999): 15.

2. Studs Terkel's foreword to Bernt Engelmann, *In Hitler's Germany: Everyday Life in the Third Reich*, trans. Krishna Winston (New York: Schocken Books, 1988), p. vii.

3. Englemann, introduction to *In Hitler's Germany*, p. xii.

4. Englemann, *In Hitler's Germany*, p. 144; compare also William L. Shirer, *The Rise and Fall of the Third Reich: A History of Nazi Germany*, new ed. (New York: Simon and Schuster, 1990).

5. Englemann, *In Hitler's Germany*, p. 196.

6. Ibid., p. 200.

CHAPTER 6

1. Kazimierz Smolen et al., *Auschwitz 1940–45: Guidebook through the Museum*, trans. Krystina Michalik (Katowice: Krajowa Agencja Wydawnicza, 1981), p. 70.

2. Ibid., p. 105.

3. Wiesenthal Center World Report, "Perspective," *Response* (winter 1999/2000): 7.

4. Ibid.

CHAPTER 7

1. Kazimierz Smolen et al., *Auschwitz 1940–45: Guidebook through the Museum*, trans. Krystina Michalik (Katowice: Krajowa Agencja Wydawnicza, 1981), p. 27.

2. Ibid., p. 35.

3. Ibid., p. 37.

CHAPTER 8

1. Kazimierz Smolen et al., *Auschwitz 1940–45: Guidebook through the Museum*, trans. Krystina Michalik (Katowice: Krajowa Agencja Wydawnicza, 1981), p. 90.
2. Ibid., p. 62.
3. Ibid., p. 73.
4. Ibid., p. 94.
5. Ibid., p. 19.
6. Ibid., p. 21.

CHAPTER 9

1. Compare the next chapter for more details.
2. Remember from chapter 2 that Himmler and other Nazi leaders boasted that they could identify a Jewish person from a distance of 50 meters.

CHAPTER 11

1. Paul Nettl, *National Anthems*, 2d enl. ed., trans. Alexander Gode (New York: Frederick Unger, 1967), 64f.
2. Franklin H. Littell, "Sirens of the Night," *Temple University Alumni Review* (winter 1979): 14.
3. Nettl, *National Anthems*, p. 88.
4. Ibid., p. 69.
5. Ibid., p. 38.
6. Ibid., p. 138.
7. Ibid., p. 203.
8. Compare Harold Bloom, *The Anxiety of Influence: A Theory of Poetry* (New York: Oxford University Press, 1972).

CHAPTER 12

1. Kazimierz Smolen et al., *Auschwitz 1940–45: Guidebook through the Museum*, trans. Krystina Michalik (Katowice: Krajowa Agencja Wydawnicza, 1981), p. 33.

2. Ibid., p. 31.

3. Ibid., pp. 31–32.

4. For details about the fate of my grandmother and the rest of the Jewish community in her hometown, see Heinrich Dittmar and Herbert Jäkel, *Geschichte der Juden in Alsfeld* (Alsfeld—Verlag Ehrenklau: Geschichts-und Museumsverein Alsfeld, 1988).

5. A caption in Rudolf Höss, *Death Dealer: The Memoirs of the SS Komandant at Auschwitz*, ed. Steven Paskuly, trans. Andrew Pollinger (Amherst, N.Y.: Prometheus Books, 1992), p. 211, misquotes ARBEIT MACHT FREI as WAHRHEIT MACHT FREI.

CHAPTER 14

1. John Loftus and Mark Aarons, *The Secret War against the Jews* (New York: St. Martin's, 1994), p. 331f.

2. Ibid., p. 506.

3. Ibid., p. 498.

4. This is also mentioned in Wiesenthal Center World Report, "Middle East," *Response* (winter 2000/2001): 4–7.

5. A British diplomat's recent term, quoted in *Voice* (December 2002): 4.

6. Mandell Ganchrow, Caption under His Photo, *Rockland Jewish Reporter*, October 23, 2000, p. 4.

7. Wiesenthal Center World Report, "Middle East," p. 6.

8. Ibid., p. 7.

Frequently Used Abbreviations and Foreign Words

GESTAPO (Geheime Staats-Polizei, Secret National Police), the dreaded head organization of the spy system.

KAPO (origin Italian), prisoner supervising a group of concentration camp inmates and work gangs; also KAPO (Konzentrationslager Polizei).

KZ Konzentrationslager

Lebensborn (Font of Life), Breeding Farm of maximum numbers of Nordic, Aryan babies, especially for future regiments.

LULOV and ETROG: palm-leaves and lemon, growth of the Jewish homeland.

MEZUZAH (pl. Mezuzoth) Hebrew doorpost attachment containing Deut. 6.4–9 and 11.13–21.

NSDAP (National-Sozialistische Deutsche Arbeiter-Partei, Nazi German Workers Party), a must for "any one who holds or seeks a job."

SA (Sturmabteilung or storm troopers). Also called "brownshirts." The SA was the original main force of the Nazi militia. The organization was later eclipsed by the SS.

SD (Sicherheitsdienst, Security Service), the widespread net of spies responsible to the SS and the Gestapo.

SS (Schutzstaffel Protective Service), Commanded by Himmler. Directly responsible for the protection of Hitler and his cohorts and other high-ranking officers.

WORKS CITED

Dittmar, Heinrich, and Herbert Jäkel. *Geschichte der Juden in Alsfeld*. Alsfeld—Verlag Ehrenklau: Geschichts-und Museumsverein Alsfeld, 1988.

Engelmann, Bernt. *In Hitler's Germany: Everyday Life in the Third Reich*. With a Foreword by Studs Terkel. Translated from German by Krishna Winston. New York: Schocken Books, 1988.

Ganchrow, Mandell. Caption under His Photograph. *The Rockland Jewish Reporter*, October 23, 2000, 4.

Hitler, Adolf. *Mein Kampf*. 2 Vols. in One. Unabridged. Munich: Verlag Franz Eher Nachfolger, 1932.

Höss, Rudolf. *Death Dealer. The Memoirs of the SS Kommandant at Auschwitz*. Edited by Steven Paskuly. Translated by Andrew Pollinger. Amherst, N.Y.: Prometheus Books, 1992.

Kershaw, Ian. *Hitler: 1889–l936 Hubris*. New York: W. W. Norton & Co., 1999.

Littell, Franklin H. "Sirens in the Night." *Temple University Alumni Review* (winter 1979): 13–15.

Loftus, John, and Mark Aarons. *The Secret War against the Jews*. New York: St. Martin's Press, 1994.

Nettl, Paul. *National Anthems* 2d enl. ed. Translated by Alexander Gode. New York: Frederick Unger, 1967.

Pessin, Deborah. *The Jewish People*. Book Three. Illustrated by Ruth Levin. New York: United Synagogue of America, 1953.

Reed, W. L., and N. J. Bristol. *National Anthems of the World*. 9th ed. London: Wellington House, 1997.

Shirer, William L. *The Rise and Fall of the Third Reich: A History of Nazi Germany*. New ed. New York: Simon and Schuster, 1990.

Smolen, Kazimierz, et al. *Auschwitz 1940–45: Guidebook through the Museum*. Trans. from Polish by Krystina Michalik. Katowice: Krajowa Agencja Wydawnicza, 1981. References to Rudolf Höss's *Reminiscences* are included. (Flyers illustrating cans containing Cyclon B were distributed at the Museum Site.)

Suchy, Barbara. "Düsseldorf: Im Jubeljahr 1988." Pamphlet Issued in Suburban Himmelgeist, 1988: 110–18.

Wiesenthal Center World Report. *Response* "History" (summer/fall 1999): 15; "Perspective" (winter 1999/2000): 6–7; "Middle East" (winter 2000/2001): 4–7.

INDEX OF NAMES

Baeck, Leo, 15

Balfour, Arthur Lord, 113, 114

Belzer, Nissan, 128

Ben-Gurion, David, 117, 120

Brod, Max, 134

Buber, Martin, 134

Busoni, Ferrucio Benvenuti, 141

Churchill, Winston Leonard Spenser, Sir, 67

Cohen, Samuel, 128

Coleridge, Samuel Taylor, 67

Dante, Alighieri, 156

David (king), 156

Dietrich, Marlene, 61, 134

Disraeli, Benjamin, Earl of Beaconsfield, 152

Dreyfus, Alfred, 113

Ebner, Gregor, 76

Eichmann, Adolf, 98

Einstein, Albert, 134

Engelmann Bernt, 69

Frederick II (king), 152

Ganchrow, Dr. Mandel, 156

Gerda (classmate), 29

Gessius Florus, 15n

Goebbels, Joseph Paul, 34

Goering, Hermann Wilhelm, 34, 70

Goethe, Johann Wolfgang, 123, 143, 152

Goldsmith, Oliver, 134

Grüspan, Herschel, 40, 56

Handel, George Frederick, 28

Haydn, Franz Joseph, 28, 122

Heine, Heinrich, 33, 56, 143
Henri (sister's husband), 63
Herzl, Theodor, 113, 114
Himmler, Heinrich, 65, 74–76, 87, 98, 156
Hindenburg, Paul von, 122
Hitler, Adolf, 13, 14, 16, 21, 23, 25, 29, 35, 40, 44, 56, 66–72, 75, 77, 109, 121, 122, 134, 136, 140, 143, 150, 151, 155
Hitler (also Hiedler, Hüttler), Alois, 13
Hoffmann von Fallersleben, August Heirtrich, 122
Hoover, Herbert, 132
Höss, Rudolph Franz Ferdinand, 54, 97, 101, 103

Ida (aunt), 23
Imber, Naftali Herz, 128
Irving, David, 156

Jabotinski, Vladimir, 114
Johnny (childhood acquaintance), 27
John Paul II, Pope, 66

Kafka, Franz, 143
Kant, Immanuel, 143
Kershaw, Ian, 13
Kohn, Professor, 30

Leibnitz, Gottfried Wilhelm, 111

Lessing, Gotthold Ephraim, 143, 152
Lipstadt, Dr. Deborah, 156
Littell, Franklin H., 122

Manfred (alias Michael Maynard), 23
Mann, Thomas, 134
Marshall, George C., 64, 77
Mendelsohn, Moses, 153
Miryam (Holocaust survivor), 95, 108
Montague, Lady, 127
Mosley, Oswald, Sir, 50, 126
Musil, Robert, 143

Niemöller, Martin, 136, 137

Owens, Jesse, 75

Pétain, Henri Philippe, 61
Pius XI, Pope, 66
Pius XII, Pope, 66, 67
Pölzl, Klara, 13

Rath, Ernst vom, 56
Rothschild, Baron de, 145
Rothschild, Max, 43
Rouget de Lisle, Claude Joseph, 123

Sam (Holocaust survivor), 92–94, 107

Sand, George, 22
Schiller, J. C. Friedrich, 143
Schlesinger, Dr. Laura, 23
Senesh, Hannah, 102

Tanik (Ted, Holocaust survivor),
    90, 92, 106, 107
Tennyson, Alfred, Lord, 121
Terkel, Studs, 68

Victoria Alexandrina (queen),
    152

Voltaire, François Marie Arouet,
    111

Waldheim, Kurt, 142
Walther von der Vogelweide, 122
Weizman, Chaim, 114, 120
Wessell, Horst, 28, 122
Windmiller family, 154